UNTRACEABL

IDENTITY

The How

Written By: J. LaStar

Dedication

I dedicate this creative piece of art I strived to start, finish and present to the world, to my son, Malachi.

You are definitely my reason for being and the light of my life! I love you with all of my heart.

I further dedicate to my god children who are an extension of me.

Also, to my nieces, nephews, and all of my greats.

ACKNOWLEDGMENTS

I have to first acknowledge every person that has told me no or I can't do something or be somebody in life. You have given me drive with no choice but to figure things out for myself. So, thank you for not coming along for this ride. Thank you for giving me space to have creative control and a voice of my own. I also wish to acknowledge the ones I have always been able to be my weird, crazy turned up self around.

Thank you to all of my people. Can't name everyone but those of you I called, bugged, hounded and exploited to gain focus and clarity through this whole process. I am forever in your debt. I am grateful to God for his grace and mercy in my life. So thank you Jesus Christ for your love and compassion.

Dear You,

You are not here by mistake. Your purpose is clear. How you feel is important and validated in every breath you take.

Here is some encouragement from Author J. LaStar, make goals, create a plan and execute it with everything you have. Show them better than you can tell them. Don't tell them because they won't understand until they see it materialized. All you need is the passion only you possess to start, and God will send you who you need to take with you on your journey.

Believe in yourself and make a habit on being honest with yourself in all things. Your vision will be clearer if you do.

Sincerely,

You

Table of Contents

F. E. A. R.

Forgetting Everything Amidst Reality

The definition of fear goes something to the effect, fear is your reaction to danger. Well now, take what makes you the most afraid and replace it with how you want to feel when you encounter that same thing.

There is a group of people who want fear to be something embraced. Something no man will be cautious of because, despite what society believes, we know the only true beauty to life is what we can see and tough. Rewriting the impact fear has on a person's confidence and trust is what drives this group to become how

5

they are. When your life is hanging in the balance, a lawyer is not going to make a case on good faith.

The members of F.E.A.R. believe that your reality and destiny is what you create. To prove your worth to anyone that counts. They further believe, your reality is your legacy which is created every day. What's in your heart doesn't play a part in your legacy. F.E.A.R. believes there is no such thing as a divined purpose just a desired one.

A cult is often associated with something you do. For a person who lives the lifestyle of any cult, they deeply believe in their heart the followings and teachings laid out for them. Their members would rather be dead than to be mediocre. In F.E.A.R. you have help and support in creating your own identity.

There is a secrecy for identities and resources requires an abundance of respect and freedom by which every rule created is to protect how F.E.A.R. operates. Therefore, there is no definition or cult associated with F.E.A.R.

Each member holds a talent or position that strengthens the glue bonding each member to uphold the rules and regulations. "Forgetting Everything Amidst Reality" strikes the pages of the book of F.E.A.R. which brands their teachings and details about the history of the beliefs. No doubting yourself because each subject holds a partnership with a major player which keeps everyone connected and respected. The members pride themselves on loyalty and respect.

In every relationship there is a dominant and a submissive. F.E.A.R. is no different, each member uses his or her connections to barter a submissive to provide their dream live. Everyone needs a partner. Every member's subject wants nothing more than to manifest their idea of success while providing the same to the member.

Since the organization is built on loyalty, your membership can only be revoked on the basis of disloyalty, doubt, and distrust in the process. Trust is a large factor. Success for those members is to leave this world knowing they made their own decisions in life. Along the way the member lives true happiness and helps one person to achieve the same.

Scrubbing identities and creating new ones is not easy. The sacrifice must be told every detail and made aware of long-term requirements such as marriage, children, castration, bodily enhancements, etc. On the other side of the coin, each perspective subject must be given the choice whether to participate or not. In the event the person starts the process in total agreement but later opts out, there are contingencies in place, which also must be agreed on if beforehand.

Each subject has been vetted, in the event one member is not a good fit, before the subject is discarded, another member can approach. After an agreement is signed there is no way to transfer it, which means the subject can only be discarded.

Diversity is low in numbers and are the demand is very high for African American woman. There are some who are always looking for those opportunities.

F.E.A.R. will soon be a gift to some and a curse to others.

CHAPTER 1 : BRUSSEL LANDS

Today was a great day to walk. New neighborhood, new school, and a new baby on the way for this beautiful family. Jasmine and Braylen walked hand in hand to the corner store. Taking in the scenery of the small Arkansas town. Although in a new place, Jasmine walked without fear. Besides, the corner store was a straight shot forward from her new home on Saint Buckingham Road in the beautiful neighborhood of Brussel Lands.

Brussel Lands is a full-on community. Small but it had just enough space for living. The corner store, named Barb's, is the only means of groceries within two miles of the intimate home ranch. Each house was separated by an alleyway barely wider than a hallway imagined to be on the inside of any one of the homes. Most houses were built identical on the outside. Judging from the looks, there was one construction company responsibility for building every home. However, the home was perfect for a beginning family.

There are trees surrounding the entire community as far as Jasmine could see. Before she purchased the home, she took a drive along the entire community at least four times. One of those times while video chatting with her husband who was overseas on one of the biggest mass deployments in U.S. history.

Brussel Lands is very beautiful. Jasmine's initial look at the home while online was breathtaking. Although the internet pictures of the community and the life here were helpful, they did not capture the still peace the trees provide. The scenery is one of the biggest reasons Jasmine fell in love with the area. The playground and children playing added to the excitement the pictures lacked. Being there and seeing what she'd seen, made Jasmine hopeful her children would be happy here.

The first time she rode through the community the trees casted its shadow on the vehicle dancing along with the speed of her car. Everything literally seemed perfect. It's still perfect on the day she decided to walk with Braylen to Barb's. It was important for him to see the community and even more important for him to know a safe place if he got lost. Jasmine's angle was for her son to see the community and know how to make it home. As many mom's do, Jasmine had an underlying agenda.

The town's people are out on their porches and playing in their yards. Some were even shouting their hello's and nice to meet you's as we walked by. There were a couple who came out to the curb to give a handshake and the really nice ones gave a hug. One can't help but to feel the good ole southern hospitality. Outside looking in, they made Jasmine feel like she belonged there.

Barb's is a small shack that looks like a building that was once a house. Very close, there is a house to the left that is fenced in. To the right of the store is a clear field. The dead grass faintly turns to gravel when it meets the front of the store. The two cars barely fitting within the gravel parking area because neither are parked straight shows how homely and comfortable the community is.

There is porch light which still burns in broad daylight. Jasmine eyes the very familiar doorbell that sits vertical the light. Surely there is no need to state the obvious that this store was once a someone's home. The door seems brand new, baring the gold and a Christmas reef which holds the letters spelling "Barb's". Jasmine pushes open the door and gives Braylen's hand a tight little squeeze. The twinkle in Braylen's eye indicates something is coming but Jerica doesn't know what. With a hint of sass, Braylen gives her hand a slight squeeze back just before reaching up to ring the doorbell. The smirk on his face causes his mom to shake her head towards him. He giggles as they work together to push the door open.

Walking into Barb's, there are a few people in line all of which have nothing in their hands. This drew Jasmine's immediate attention because it seems strange at first glance. The store walls are lined with candy, bread, chips, household cleaning supplies, toiletries and a variety of ramen noodles. There is a soda freezer off by itself in the corner barely lit. Simply organized but packed with items, just somewhere to get something very quick and that is the only way to describe this place. Braylen gets chips and a small canned soda while Jasmine stands in line to hold her place because she knows he will not be long.

After the cashier rings up the first person in line and their groceries are paid for, she listens to the next person. She doesn't take any money; she just smiles and walks away from the register. Barb disappears to a shadowy corner which seems to be a protected area. When the cashier returns from the shadow, she has something wrapped in a brown paper bag and tied with a red string.

At this point the man pays for his strange bag and leaves. Smiling proudly and holding on to Braylen's hand, Jasmine makes her way to the counter. Braylen throws his contents onto the wooden surface. "I don't believe I've had the pleasure of meeting either of you. My name is Barb and I run this joint. If you look to your left here, you will find there a list of the cigarettes, cigars, and any alcoholic beverages we have available. This list changes based on what the truck brings. You may request anything on this list from me, should you wish. No judgements. If you look on the wall to the right, you will find a list of meat we cut and sell here and the price per pound."

Barb is an elderly woman. Best guess, she is about 5'4" and about 60 years old. Her skin is slightly wrinkled but the hunch in her back gives away her age. She has a glossy gray tint to her yellow stained eyes and her hair is completely gray, which she keeps in a ponytail.

Barb hasn't taken her eyes from Jasmine the entire time she is speaking. "Well thank you for that helpful information. This is Braylen, I am Jasmine, and this here is baby Jessica and we are new here to this beautiful area. My husband Brandon is overseas fighting for his country, but you will be seeing us here very often. It's our pleasure to meet you."

Both women are smiling and giggling at each other's introduction. Barb, says through the laughter smiling with every tooth on display, "Well, pleased to meet you as well. I look forward to seeing your smiling face over and over. Is this all for you?"

"Yes, thank you. We are just out for a stroll." Jasmine says as she grabs her change. Her and Braylen walk out of the heavy door all waves and smiles.

The picture is perfect. Nothing could go

wrong as it seems. In the coming months, Jasmine gives birth to a 9-pound 3-ounce baby Jessica. Brandon returns home for next 6 months. Shortly after he is off to conquer the impossible mission of saving our world again. Afghanistan this time. Time is moving and the family is continuing every day without a worry.

Until.

CHAPTER 2 : THE THOMAS FAMILY

It has been fifteen years since Jasmine, Braylen, and baby Jessica unexpectedly disappeared. There was one lead from a woman that later passed away from natural causes. The neighbor of the Thomas family was the last person to testify seeing them alive. Miss Johnson was one of the neighborhood grandmothers. She was a grandmother to not only her own children's children but also to children that needed a grandmother or guidance or even lunch money. She was one of the purest souls in Brussel Lands, Arkansas.

Miss Johnson was the ear to the town. She didn't see much because she was always inside, but she knew everything about Brussel Lands. As the oldest tenant and homeowner in the community she was the go-to person no matter the situation.

Average height for a woman, even toned dark skin, and rings on every finger, Miss Johnson was a round elderly lady that couldn't help but give the best hugs and kisses to every child in her area. The streets have taught her survival, but she was so much more than struggle and survival, she had heart and courage. Although she was the last to set eyes on any parts of the Thomas family, no one suspected her to have harmed them. Natural curly hair layered around her face with evidence of her years in each wrinkle around her eyes and mouth, Miss Johnson wouldn't hurt a soul.

During the investigation, the police questioned everyone on the block initially. Miss Johnson gave her report of the last conversation she had with her neighbors. There was one person that Miss Johnson quietly suspected to have something to do with whatever crime took place with this family. The same one who claimed to never have spoken with the family. By his false report, when the incident occurred, he was not home.

When the authorities suggested the other neighbor has reported that was not the case, Miss Johnson' suspicions were realized. After Mr. Slack was alibied by one of his lawyer friends stating he as at a banquet dinner for the local boy scot's organization two states away. Miss Johnson knows people who kept her abreast to all details surrounding the disappearance of the Thomas family and none of them believed it one bit. Miss Johnson's disbelief was not kept quiet in the confidential settings of her own home.

Even with the most trusted account in the neighborhood, charges were never filed, and Mr. Slack was never named a person of interest. Other than Mr. Slack, the police never had any leads.

Jasmine lived on the block for about three years until tragedy struck their family. The Thomas family used to be complete with Brandon, who was Jasmine's husband and the father of her children. Brandon spent most of those three years in Afghanistan. Braylen was young but he was a little man in his own right. He loved to stay busy whether he was helping with the yard or playing baseball. He adored his mom and sister.

The reason the home was bought was because

their family was expanding. As soon as Brandon was stationed, they decided because he was going away yet again while Jasmine was pregnant his family would need to be stable. No one expected the reality that was to come. Little did Brandon or his family know he would not be returning. Brandon died during his last stint. Bombs were placed under the truck he was occupying.

Conspiracies circled. With the condition of his body he, along with 4 other members of his camp, was dismembered. Disrupting life as Jasmine knew it, her family was also dismembered. Carrying the pressure of what happened and dealing with the U.S. Government response, Jasmine weighted moving back home with her sister and giving up the house. The lack of support from the branch and the limits placed on their family due to life's tragedies began to quickly take a toll on Jasmine. Both of Brandon's parents were deceased and he was the only child of his mother and father. Her family and the pressure were just too much for Jasmine to bear alone. Shortly after Brandon's death, she decided to apply for jobs and childcare. She was giving up on the inside.

There was panic and a sense of emptiness after the news traveled to the Thomas family. That type of panic and pain never really leaves you.

The mother of two children and widow had mentally checked out. Anyone who knew her in the 3 years she had lived there in the area really felt sorry for her.

CHAPTER 3 : MISS JOHNSON

Miss Johnson's report to the police reads a play by play on her conversation with the kid and his mother as well as setting the scene for the day. Starting with Braylen's whereabouts because he is where this whole thing starts.

"Braylen was playing in the backyard. It was hot outside so there weren't many children to play with. Braylen had been an only child for a while and was used to playing by himself. He had a t ball stand and a bat set up in his backyard. There was also a volleyball net and kiddie pool. No one was available to splash in the pool considering the temperature was so hot it wasn't even safe for kids to be outside. He also didn't want to play with the volleyball net, I mean it would be exceptionally hard to hit the ball over the net and expect for it to come back when there is no one on the other side. The t-ball set is the only thing that made sense for Braylen.

I could hear him and his mom going back and forth on how unfair it was that baby Jessica wasn't old enough to play with him. He also mentioned that day that his dad would never come home and how unfair life was. I would hear him hit the ball and take off running after it. Complaining the entire time but still treating it like a game against a full team. Hitting the ball softly, he would take off running to go get the ball as soon as the bat fell to the ground. It was quite entertaining to listen to."

Miss Johnson vividly tells the story as she remembers it to paint a perfect picture to the Crittenden County Police Department accompanied by the Brussel Lands Police Department.

"Braylen thought he heard the sound of kids playing. I know that because I thought I heard some too and was getting excited for the boy. Stopping in his tracks as he looked around, but the sounds stopped. The next time Braylen hit the ball he used all the force in his little body. I take it he was a little upset about there being no other children outside to play with. The ball goes over the fence.

Braylen runs in the house to tell his mother the ball had been hit over the fence.

"When Jasmine got to my door her hands were wet and she had an apron on. Baby Jessica's shirt was filthy, but her face and hands were clean. Looks like Braylen interrupted feeding and cleaning time. Jasmine asked me about the ball but after looking at every detail in my backyard to be sure, we concluded that the ball was not here. Last I heard from Jasmine, she was headed next door to Jonathan's doorstep. There has been no sign of her since that day. About two hours later, through my window, I heard Braylen speaking to someone. I could hear a man's voice. Since we were positioned so far apart from each other, I could barely hear."

"Because I am hard of hearing, I cannot confirm who came to the door or what happened after that point."

The police left the block spending less and less time at each of the other houses. There was very little information to go on. The investigation only lasted the better part of thirty days. That is the last time any parts of this family were heard of again.

Over time evidence of the Thomas family's existence seemed to disappear. Before her sudden death, Miss Johnson asked one of her many grandchildren who was a part of their local city hall office to look into the case. She was curious and wanted an update on the progress. There was no shame in calling Malachi. School records, bank accounts, debt, everything had disappeared. Her grandson could not give her any information. He was even at one point skeptical that the records were off limits to the public because of the computer glitch that occurred while he conducted his small investigation. The computer shut down while the file downloaded. Malachi ended up having to get another computer because his would not come back on. Miss Johnson's connections had no information on the case of the Thomas Family.

Miss Johnson had only asked because Jasmine had one sister that she was concerned with helping. The one sister was determined to find out what happened to her niece, nephew and most importantly her sister. Lack of information or facts and no leads never stopped Jasmine's sister, Doris, from continuously asking questions and coming around. Hanging flyers and knocking on doors, Doris would get the same answer from everyone on the block, no one had further information.

She came by to each house asking the same questions to anyone who made eye contact. "Have you seen my family? Has anyone besides me come by asking about them? Have you heard any new details from your own family and friends? Has anyone else gone missing since my family has? Will you call me at this number if you find out anything else?"

People were never rude to Doris because they all understood the pain she was in. Everyone wished they could help her in some way. The small community never dealt with such a tragedy. Most people couldn't fathom having such a monster so close and didn't want to believe it was possible something bad happened while she and the kids were home.

As far as the community knew Jasmine and the kids vanished without a trace. Doris came back once a week, pounding the pavement anyhow. Once a week, every single week, until Miss Johnson passed away. After that one day you seen her and no one realized, but it would have been the last time. No one else ever asked any questions or even gave Doris the time of the day to address any of her concerns. Besides, the community was filled with longtime friends and extremely close family members. The Thomas family was from an outside world the small town had no clue about. Jasmine's family were classified as outsiders.

Weeks to come, in the still of the late evening children in every yard playing without a care in the world. Just a regular day in the neighborhood. Cars slowly circling the block with music playing just loud enough for porch watchers to hear what's on. The drivers smiling and bobbing their head to their own music. From every porch, neighbor's TV's all echo each other with BREAKING NEWS!!!!!

The televisions all sound off. Neighbors only listen. No one in this tight knit community has to pay a lot of attention. Detailing the door being left wide open, food cooking on the stove, the smell of burnt bread and a family whom vanished without a trace. No need to look at the recurring news clips, neighbors' testimonies and repeat articles to inform the community that there are still no leads. Those are paid to report and others who are still concerned with the story of the Thomas Family invade every listening ear.

News reporters desperately beg for tips or more information at least 4 times every day. The news reports the entire community have seen so many times reminding them of the nice family's disappearance and the mysteries surrounding each detail. Sadness crosses the faces of those who have ever spoken with or got to know the family even in the smallest of ways.

It's been a month since the Thomas family's disappearance. The home was more than likely taken by the bank or someone of that nature because a new family was moving in shortly after we heard the last sounds of, "Please, if you have any information regarding the whereabouts of Jasmine, Braylen and baby Jessica Thomas, please call the tips hotline, we just want them back, please."

No more sounds, no more news articles, many remembers but no one speaks of the family that once occupied 21 Buckingham Rd. Brussel Lands, AR 72300. Life went on.

15

YEARS LATER

CHAPTER 4 : HELP ME

In the dead of the night. A passerby thinks he heard something in the distance. As he approaches a location three streets over from his destination, smoke fogs the area. A dangerous quiet fall on Buckingham Road. The passerby's voice echoes after an apparent crash. The man grabs his dirt stained hat and turns it backwards in distress. "There was an accident." The man's strained words weigh heavily in the air. With heavy sighs he stresses through the phone. "Car accident. One car, driver only no passengers." Walking towards the other car, the passerby barely audible. "Second car, one driver two passengers, children, there is one in a car seat one not." The passerby recounts to dispatch.

Long dark hair stuck to her face soaked by the blood nearly gushing as it spills from her forehead, lip and nose. Her almond-colored skin is slightly illuminated from the streetlights. Her bright green shirt and powder blue jeans all splattered with blood making them discolored. Her hands are dropped to her side bruised from the force of the air bag. Voices are close and shouting. "I think she is still alive." The passerby sounds distraught and anxious. "Hold on we are going for help." He taps on the glass as he continues to talk painfully loud to her.

"Jerica, wake up. Jerica you're hurt. Please hear my voice, get up, you're hurt." Blinking to consciousness the woman opens her eyes looking for her sister Jameria's voice. Holding her neck unable to stand the pain, Jerica fully open her eyes. With heavy breathing, she starts to moan. "Wait, what happened?" Unanswered questions arise as she is trying to move her legs. "Oh God, no." Her words not forming sentences, as she starts to twist in her seat to undo the seat belt that binds her. Finally, words stagger from Jerica's mouth that make sense. "Is everyone ok?" Jerica begins to look around and to her surprise no Jameria. She gets out of the car stumbling taking note of all her visible injuries. Falling towards the other vehicle, still mumbling, Jerica is disoriented but she can still see that the woman in the driver's seat is unresponsive with visible injuries as well.

Both cars are still connected to each other. The voices that were heard are all gone. Jerica's car is an old, white 1988 two door cavalier. The shape of her trunk is unrecognizable due to the other car still holding it tight in place from the accident. Jerica's car was lodged under the front of the SUV.

There is a vent window that is open just enough to get her arm through. Reaching out to the dark-haired stranger, Jerica is gentle while shaking the woman trying to get her to open her eyes. Her body is pressed up against the steering wheel and there is lots of blood dripping from somewhere. "Wake up, we are hurt. Can you hear me? You have to wake up." The woman is not responding to Jerica's cries or the cries of her children.

Jerica peeks through the back window of the banged-up car connected to hers. There are children in the seat. One of the children is screaming from her car seat, while the older kid is rummaging through a bag screaming for his unresponsive mother. Every one of the windows are up. Jerica is cries out in desperation to the child, "I'm going to get help. Please don't leave the car." Her words are so muffled she doesn't think the child can even hear her. On que milli seconds before she began knocking again, the boy looks up at Jerica with a busted head and tears in his eyes. He shakes his head slowly up and down in an ok motion acknowledging her.

Jerica has no strength to tap on the glass again. She slowly turns towards the empty street behind her. Feeling weak and lightheaded, Jerica takes one last look at the mother in the front seat. She still hasn't woken up. Tears stream down Jerica's face as she realizes the children's mother is probably deceased. Instantly saddened and drained all at once, the only response to everything around her Jerica can muster to say is, "oh no."

Taking into a mental account her surroundings, she finds there is only light in one direction. Jerica still disoriented with blurred vision, wonders to the first house with a porch light. Wary, the woman found the steps lined by two banisters and slowly perched herself up each one until she made it to the top landing. Falling as if in the arms of the one she loved, she loses her balance and slams her body on the door frame.

CHAPTER 5 : CAN YOU HEAR ME

Jerica listens while her head is resting on the door pane. Waiting to see if she hears anything on the other side of the door. In her mind, Jerica is impatient and wills herself to start ringing the doorbell again. The doorbell was not sounding off as fast as she hit the button. To attempt to create a bigger disturbance, she decided to try to say something in hopes someone might hear. As soon as she began to speak, Jerica hears the lock clink and the knob twist. There was a very unattractive face who appeared in the doorway. A man. He had wrinkles and sunken eyebrows, wild gray hair and golden eyes. He's staring at Jerica cold and very hard. This man towered over her poor broken and bruised body. It hurts to turn her head, but she manages. Squinting her eyes, she barely had enough strength to think, let alone keep her head lifted while the large overhead tortures her. Body limp and resting on the door frame is taking some of the pressure off of her knees. Jerica started to speak but no words would form. She cleared her throat several times but there is not a drop of moisture there. Her eyes are tired, and her vision is still badly blurred. She dropped her head to release some pressure from her neck and whispered as loud as she could and prayed that out loud her words were heard by the giant before her.

At this moment someone began to speak to Jerica and as the pain shot sharply through her neck, she managed to still lift her head towards the voice. Behind the old grumpy face another face appears. In Jerica's dry throat she is talking nonstop but it doesn't appear either of the men hear her. Both of them are staring at her without blinking, without speaking, and she doesn't have the strength to get mad. The younger guy has much softer features and he even spoke calmly. "Come." With that single word Jerica began to step forward into the house as the sweet-faced man took her hand. The old man hands her a miniature bottle of water. He tilts her head back and slowly pours. Once she completed the bottle, her eyes at the young stranger's eyes as her neck protested.

Starting her rant all over again Jerica is confident this time they can hear her. "My name is Jerica and there has been an accident." As Jerica spoke the tall man coaxed her to a soft chair sitting in the corner near the door she just walked through. Once she is settled in the light brown armchair, she tries to make sense of her twisted and confusing language. What she wills her mouth to say is not the words she put together in her mind to say. Even slowing down and taking deep breaths was not helping her. The young man takes one hand and places it on Jerica's shoulder to calm. She starts over and manages to tell them, "There are 2 small children in the other vehicle, please call the police we all need an ambulance." Jerica continues in a low, breathy voice as her eyes run from the old man to the young man. The old man handed her another small bottle of water.

The young mountain man looks into Jerica's eyes. She starts to feel a sense of accomplishment when it appears, he has been listening to her. The man speaks pointedly in her direction and very attentively, "Jerica, my name is Jonathan and you are safe." As soon as he spoke, she is taken aback so quickly she spits out much of the water Jerica blurts out in the middle of Jonathan's statement, "so you can hear me!" Jonathan continues, "Calm down, we will take care of you." Looking into Jonathan's eyes Jerica says out loud, "Thank God, you can hear me."

As Jerica is shushed and calmed by Jonathan's young face and smooth voice, she notices the man with no words has disappeared. Moments later Jerica realizes she has been paying close attention to Jonathan, and talking nonstop to this calm, mountain of a man that the old man, may not have been there the entire time. Suddenly the grumpy old man walks in the door with one baby girl and one boy child. Trying to focus blinking rapidly, Jerica is brought back to her senses taking initiative to control the situation as she seems to always do ash asked, "have you called the police yet?" No one answers. Jerica becomes very panicked.

She sees the grumpy old man gently dragging the older kid and carrying the younger child. The baby is quiet, but the other kid is the one kicking and screaming. Seeing the child fight brings Jerica back to what's happened. From the looks of things everyone in this situation is at the mercy of grumpy old man, which seems to be making all decisions, and his sidekick. The troubling thing is the younger guy's attention is only the children. But why? She turns to Jonathan waving her hands and raising her voice asking him what his aim is. "What do you get out of all this? Why us?" With a protesting neck and back, Jerica's outburst is not responded to by neither of the abductors. She grabs on to Jonathan's chest muscles while grabbing his shirt. Dizzy at a moment's notice, Jerica clutches his shirt in her fist.

Without warning, darkness takes over before the words can release from her mouth and swim around her thoughts. She can't see but her senses are screaming something is wrong. Jerica opens her eyes to find she is sitting in the armchair "what's happening? I need help. Can someone hear me? I need your help."

Next to the man that called himself Jonathan. There's a picture hanging on the wall. It looks like it could be one of those annoying memes that seems to repetitively travel on social media. It's the old man but younger. He has his palm open and the words are in a way sitting midair like magic above his hand. "F. E. A. R." Even as a young man, he still looks mean. Just like fear personified. The caption at his feet reads, "Forgetting everything you think you know amidst the reality you create to achieve your own idea of what success looks like. Giving you the power to create and maintain your own idea of what independent happiness is."

Smoke fills the space and noises start to happen. Oxygen is leaving her body, so she begins to breathe heavily. Beyond every emotion she is feeling right now, there is a faint sound laughing and music. Panic sets in as the confusing unease of the dark place that surrounds Jerica invites a reaction. "Who is that laughing?" Jerica tried to turn around to see where the noise is coming from and she's restrained. Her heavy breaths get deeper and more restrained. Jerica continues her line of question, "Where is that noise coming from? I don't see what's funny."

Jumping like a fish out of water, Jerica is brought to her present. She's brought somewhere familiar. She starts to grip her chest as she realizes how calm she is becoming. "It's all a bad dream." There is a hundred people around and they are all having lots of fun. Looking from face to face around the room, she finds her sister Jameria's small face "lit up like Christmas in Memphis" as our grandma used to say.

Off in the background there is an unfamiliar voice, "Doctor, is she completely under?" The voice sounds worried and maybe even scared. "Yes, you may start questioning her now." Jerica is looking for someone in the crowd that could be talking. "She's dreaming about something pleasant. I can tell." Jonathan is observing Jerica as she sleeps. "Tell me what you see." He whispers in her ear.

Jerica is feeling a little anxious because she recognizes the voice of Jonathan from her dreams. She doesn't see him anywhere which makes her feel calm again. "I'm heading over here to the lawn chairs by this group of tables." There are people everywhere, but no one responds to her. "If anyone cares." She adds with a hint of attitude with her volume slightly raised.

"A screeching noise from the distance grabs Jerica's attention as she jumps to her feet. "Jerica! Jerica!" my little sister is yelling as she begs me to help her figure out where the pinata is so she can be the lucky one to spill its contents. She is blindfolded but can't wait to see what could be treats or what could be tricks our parents are hiding as she continuously cries my name. We are attending the annual Halloween block party. All of the old folks throw this party to relive their childhood glory days during the holiday season. They compete baked goods and show off old clothes. The lights are all flickering lightly but stop."

Jonathan wants to know more. "Tell me how you feel." Jerica obliges. "Not really paying close attention to the lighting. I'm happy we are having fun. This feels good. These parties are always the highlight of our lives too, I must admit."

Jonathan says, "I want to share your happiness, keep going what's happening now?" There is no hesitation from Jerica to continue describing one of the best times in her life. "Jam-Jam, it's to your left." I yell to assist her, knowing if I don't, she will never forgive me. Around the circle of children, they are all looking angrily at me. "Better you mad than her." I say to everyone staring me down displeased. She swings missing it completely. Turning herself as she continues to swing the large stick to her left. In my opinion she is still dizzy from how many times they spun her around in the beginning. Again, what's up with the lights still flickering. This time the residence lights, and the streetlights are all flickering, but no one seems to notice it but me. A few moments later the lights are flickering rapidly. "What is happening?"

"Something's wrong doctor, wake her up

now." Jonathan is barely containing her anger.

Startled, Jerica wakes up breathing extremely heavy, cold sweats and touching all over her body to see if she still has all her fingers and toes. There is a huge mirror on the wall in front of her. Her eye is caught because the mirror exposed her dramatics. Seeing her reflection brings a moment of truth to her. Tears unprovoked starts to stream down her face.

It's a sad time while she watches herself in the mirror until she gains the courage to turn away.

Jerica watches a tear splatter on the comforter. She's drawn to notice her clothes are different and both children are beside her crying. Jerica reaches out to them. First grabbing the baby girl. It's not rocket science to know this baby is missing something in her life. She's unhappy. As the precious little baby found a comfortable place to lay, bottom lip slightly quivered. With clinched fists, she rubs both eyes. Jerica whispers a word of comfort, "I think you are calming down now. Its ok, I'm here."

That tall mountain climbing man walks in looking around the room for lord knows what. As her attention is drawn to him, Jerica notices a few more features. While blinking to full consciousness after the bright light from the hallway fills the entrance of the room, there is one feature in particular that attracts Jerica's attention. Jonathan is a silver fox. Standing in the doorway only for a second, Jonathan walks in slowly and with one swift and less than gentle move he grabs the now quiet baby from tucked by Jerica's side. The older boy throws a fit. Crying harder and louder, the young boy screams for his sister. Attempting to soothe him and inwardly questioning what the man will do or has done with either of these children she tries to calm the boy by reaching for him.

In his cry Jerica hears love and pain. It's very disheartening. With gentle ease Jerica, rubs the child's soft hair on his head. He is calming down but while she attends to him, she can see Jonathan is walking back and forth in the hallway past the room bouncing the baby up and down. She feels the child's hand reach to cradle, the small grooves of her back and then holding her close.

Looking from one child to the doorway, Jerica is trying to quickly understand what is happening in this moment. She isn't supposed to have those children. She's not strong enough. Jonathan disappears from sight with the baby. He leaves Jerica and the young boy laying side by side in the small bed. Jonathan didn't so much as acknowledge either one of their presence. Jerica puts her arm around the small boy to console him returning her attention to obvious small show of affection. His grip gets tighter and her heart starts to bleed for him. Jerica begins to turn her body so she's cuddling him. In doing so, her foot brushes a large book that is clinging to the foot of the bed. Briefly glancing, careful not to take too much attention from the young child and careful not to strain her neck too much, she sees it reads "F. E. A. R." Making the connection she whispers to herself, "just like the one in the front".

CHAPTER 6 : MICHAEL

No more tears to cry. Staring into space as she rocks the young boy back and forth. Her flashback is fuzzy, but Jerica remembers the accident. The memory playing shows highlights of the kids, and the lady that appeared to be dead, the position of the cars and the porch light. Multiple voices yelling out about the accident and Jerica's freaking out as she sits on the armchair. She tries to get up but is very weak from the doctored injuries that are still apparently affecting her. Looking into the eyes of the young boy beside her, she aimed to start slow as she began asking questions.

"Hey buddy, I need to ask you some questions that may be uncomfortable for you to think about." At no surprise to her, all she can get is a shoulder shrug from him and that is good enough for her.

She continues to look for answers in his eyes. "Were the police called?" The boy shrugs his shoulders again. This time with a very disturbed look on his face as if searching her eyes for an answer.

"Ok buddy, did you just wake up too?" Never having had a relationship with a child so young before, Jerica asks to lighten the load. "No, I can't sleep." He buries his head deeper in Jerica's top breast area and snuggles to her closer. "Let's get to know each other." He has an interested smile on his face now. "How old are you?" Without hesitation he answers, "eleven".

Jerica decides to take one more stab at trying to see what he knows. "Have you seen your mom since you've been here?" There is a less than chipper answer, but he answers the question no less. "No, I don't know where she went." This time she decides to scale it back. "What's your name son?" His eyes met hers once again. "Michael"

There is now a relaxed tone to his anxiety and unease. Either that or he is finally getting in position to sleep. Michael is getting sleepy or he is really relaxed. His head is snuggled while his feet are curled near his butt, making his knees naturally rest on top of Jerica. "Do you know how many days we have been here, Michael?" "Four days," he says without moving from his safe space.

After the short questionnaire Jerica's mind is working overtime but Michael is peaceful and quiet. "Michael, I need to speak to Jonathan. I have to call him in." The young boy says nothing. His blank stare doesn't hide the confused emotion this eleven-year-old that is feeling. Careful not to prolong the inevitable so in an instant Jerica starts screaming out for Jonathan. When he entered the room his first words were, "Please keep the noise down, baby Sapphire just went to sleep." Michael is looking dangerously at the tower of a man standing before them, so Jerica followed suit.

The two adults and one child in the room glare at each other for about thirty seconds before someone decides to speak. "Yes, ma'am, what do you want?" Jonathan's voice is low and tired, but Jerica can almost catch the sarcasm in her hand.

In a respectful tone, Jerica starts demanding to know what is going on. "Why haven't any of us been taken to the hospital to be checked out?"

Jonathan's face is tired, eyes are sunken, and there is no life in his voice. He is staring Jerica in the eyes as he stands before her bed as she clutches Michael just as tight as he is holding onto her. She can feel her blood beginning to boil undoubtedly because she has not gotten an answer. Knowing Michael doesn't appreciate being shuffled aside but Jerica stands ignoring her pain and protesting limbs. Her hair is a mess and whatever nightgown she has on doesn't seem to be hers. Jerica knows confidence, if she was never taught anything else, she knows how to stand her ground in complete confidence.

The night down is much too wide and much too short for her comfort. The color is a hunter green that shimmers so its attention grabbing. Forgetting her weaknesses, she stands tall, shoulders are squared and face in an unwavering mug. She cocks her head to one side and exclaims in a deliberate sass, "Well?" Her one-word question was about to be answered until there was a knock at the door.

Jonathan turns to walk away. He takes one step from the door as she screams out "I have more questions." Jerica doesn't know where in the house she is. The voices at the door are moving farther and farther away as Jonathan pulls the door closed. "Obviously not at the moment you don't." Jonathan manages to keep speaking but his voice is disappearing as the door closes.

Jerica jumped up and down in one spot yelling as loud as her banged up body would allow. "We're here, we're here". Starting to run and charge forward, she is halted by her restraints. Jerica, at this moment, realized she is bound and is down faster than she knew what was happening. "I'm tied up! Let me out!" Returning the sarcasm given from him before, Jerica begins taunting Jonathan for his decision to bind her. "What type of animal am I huh? A dog? A rabbit pit-bull? Oh, maybe a llama or a tiger? I hate you." Jonathan returns from somewhere in the hallway. Him standing there and takes every harsh word without flinching as if he'd heard it all before, is making Jerica even madder.

An extremely exhausted eleven-year-old traumatized by all he's been through turns aggressive. Michael drops his head down letting out a growl to initiate a collection of words that grabs both Jerica and Jonathan's attention. "I've tried that. It doesn't work. Nothing works!" The young boy turns his back to both Jonathan and Jerica slamming his body into the mattress. Jonathan looks Jerica squarely in the eyes and whispers, "I have acquired by all means necessary, a wife, son and baby I just fed and laid down for a nap." Walking from the room, Jonathan closes the door smiling despite his obvious lack of sleep as if that is to explain what's transpired.

Michael gets up to crack the door and scurries back to his side of the bed. Furious but the only emotion shown is the few tears falling slowly down her face. Again, she hears a knock at the door, only this time, she says nothing. She can hear a male voice say "We are here investigating a possible accident. Wanting to find out if you know of or have direct knowledge of anything. There is a guy claiming he may have seen an accident, but we have no evidence of or any leads for this accident." Tuning out the rest of the conversation because the voices are faint meaning Jonathan probably took them outside and closed the door. "I wonder who could have seen the accident. Someone out there knows something. There is no way they can keep us here." Michael slowly turns to look at Jerica with clear evidence he had been crying. He says nothing and he doesn't have to.

Jonathan appears back in the room with an angered look on his face. Not knowing what to expect Jerica jumps up off of the mattress and plants her feet in the ground ready for anything. Same stance as before, Jerica is back toe to toe with the giant, Jerica is met with his agitated gaze. She searches his eyes for whatever question he seems to be asking as they stare each other down yet again. She, with the look of anger and Jonathan with something else, reaches around and snatches Michael without a word and drags him away covering his mouth. Jerica starts to protest but doesn't want to be the cause of Michael being hurt. The possibilities are just too hard to bear. Jerica screams "where are you taking him." The innocent sweet face Michael has, has been given by God and doesn't deserve mistreatment of any kind. He has been through enough. By his own admission he is concerned about his mom, his crying for his sister shows his compassion and his protective nature. Jerica refuses to be a part of his abuse.

Peeking through the thin slot just below the top hinge as the door closes, Jerica can see the grumpy faced man looking as angry as ever. He grabbed hold of Michael's hand and take him in the room across from hers. He is protesting and fighting but Michael is no match for the old man. Without even a flinch, Michael is unsuccessful and out of sight. Jonathan comes back into the room where Jerica is kept. Standing too close to her, towering over her, staring once again into her eyes. "What did you do to Michael?" The mountain man says nothing. "We will get out of here; you just wait and see." He takes a step closer to Jerica and speaks in a tone too hard for her to hear. "By any means necessary." Jerica feels a prick and before she can fight it, darkness takes over yet again.

"Someone with cold hands is poking and touching me. I can't open my eyes. My eyes don't work. Can you hear me? Stop touching me." Jerica is screaming profusely. "Where are we going." Kicking, she is being drug through the woods by a heavily covered person. This person is covered in dark rags that scrape the ground. She's screaming at the top of her lungs. There are large amounts of grass, then mud, water, more grass, then dirt. While hitting every tree root that is growing on top of the ground it's hard to get a grip on anything. Her words leave but she is alert to what is going on. She is screaming nonstop but where are her words. She cannot hear herself screaming anymore. In the midst of all going on Jerica began to start thinking out loud. "If my words are gone and not even, I can hear myself it's not impossible that you can even hear me." Suddenly the man dragging her stops and turns to face her. His face is covered and after a second, he turns around and starts back dragging her. "Where are we going?" She screams but he doesn't stop. There is still a deafness and she can't hear herself talk. Someone else is here and starts running beside the covered man.

Now, there are two people ahead of her. Efforts still go unnoticed for someone to hear her lost words. All that's left to do is fight. Trying to snatch her foot away, she's twisting and turning herself into a pretzel. Aimed to move faster than they can control, Jerica is trying to grab hold of something to help stop herself. Instead, her plan backfires.

She's tossed into the air and gets a glimpse of the horrible creature kidnapping her. There is a familiar shape to head. Jerica tries to stop herself once again so that she can get another glimpse. In her repetitive bumping she gains sight of a branch that's coming up. In one calculated move, Jerica grabs hold to the branch to try to stop herself once again. The plan once again backfires and tosses Jerica into the air.

She screams out, "monsters". With a side glance, Jerica is sure it's her father. The person beside him is her mother. Both are covered with unidentified items. The second slow fall also allows Jerica to take a closer look at the top layer of garments draped over their heads.

Newspapers. "Mom! Dad! Wait! Where is Jam? Where are you taking me?" Something has happened and she can feel it. "Wait, tell me what's wrong. Tell me what to do." She plead in screams for their attention, but she still isn't listened to. Jerica fights to wake up. Fights to open her eyes. Her body hits the soft ground over and over. Her screams are muffled. Her parents halt without warning. At this time Jerica has tears falling from her eyes. Beat up and abandoned by life her feelings are hurt. "Please, mom. Dad?" Her sobs are harder once she realizes they won't answer back. Her father turns to her and says, "stop doing nothing". Both her mom and dad take her body and swing Jerica by her legs towards a shadowy corner. Before she hits what maybe a brick wall, she jerks awake.

CHAPTER 7 : LIVING QUARTERS

Jerica opens her eyes and yet again her clothes are changed. Rubbing and touching herself from top to bottom to make sure she is not injured more than what she had been. Her senses are slowly awakening. "I feel better." Waking up this time is different for her. There's been some moving around and some cleaning. Sniffing and trying to catch the smell, she is smelling cleaning supplies. "Pine sol, bleach and fabulosos". She whispers as she remembers the familiar items often used the when helping her mom clean for years after her father passed. "It's not clean unless you can verify it with your nose." Jerica recalls her mom's saying out loud. Those smells never really leave a person.

Jerica is looking around the room in stunned confusion. Before when the room was dark and her body was in pain, thoughts of looking around had never crossed her mind. Seeing wouldn't have done any good when the feeling of being here was so overwhelming for Jerica. Speaking without thinking, Jerica connects the dots as she understands the situation. "Now that I am thinking about it, either the room changed or everything I've felt around the room was me demonizing the demon. There definitely wasn't a clean smell or even a lighted area anywhere."

Where she was before, was dark and unbecoming. She was tied to the bed and that is all she could focus on. Dismissing what she really couldn't even remember, the young captive took in the sites. Where she's being held has no windows but have 2 pictures of windows. There is an old-fashioned spider lamp with flowers as the light bulb housing. "Scary and old fashioned." Jerica says out loud knowing she is talking to herself.

Her voice is strained and light. Her eyes continue their inspection of the surroundings with quiet gratefulness that she can see her mind may have played a trick or two on her. With no excitement in her voice she declares, "this is not a dungeon". The walls are papered with a light blue and yellow striped pattern. There is what looks like about a 70-inch screen television, black in color inside a shiny oak wood entertainment center. Surround sound speakers, DVD player, Blu-ray player and stereo all organized in a flashy kind of way covering the entire corner inside and all around the television. The electronics are all black with red and yellow flashing lights. The lights flashing is blurry.

Jerica blinks a few times to try to see better but give up. Sitting up in bed a little taller she is able to see a little better. The bed Jerica is fastened to is made of oak wood as well. Stained in a deep brown, light brown and black speckles just like the entertainment center. A floral-patterned light blue and yellow bedspread which matches almost perfectly with the walls and overall ambiance of the room covers the bed Jerica is bound to. She has six pillows, two decorative and four with pillow slips to match the bedspread. The small fashionable bed is accompanied by one tall dresser, nightstand and a rocking chair. Glancing at everything not spending much time, all are either completely covered in same stained wood look or trimmed in the same manner. The drawers on the tall dresser are all knobbed with block squares which seem to be out of place. The jewelry box oddly so looks just like the dresser it's housed on.

Beside the bed there's a nightstand. On top sits a bible and a lamp both the same shade of blue that again matches the shade on the walls. The lamp shade is beige which matches but is very different from anything else in that room.

Jerica breath catches as she notices the old grumpy faced man staring at her in amusement. Besides droopy and very unbecoming, this man's smile seeps right through to the pit of Jerica's stomach with a lingering disgust. Looking at him is like living in a horror movie for her. Sitting there across from him, she is trying to decide whether or not to waste time speaking to a man that cannot speak back. He is looking back as if he were an artifact in a museum that has been in the same position for thousands of years. He sits as if he has been placed in a very particular way to protect the museum from evil spirits past. After a few seconds of dead stares accompanied by dead silence Jerica speaks out with aggravation and a massive attitude, "where is Jonathan?" The man gets up from the chair as slowly as he can muster with a hint of pleasure because he is reading Jerica's annoyance in her voice and on her face as he leaves the room. She watches after him.

Before she starts throwing a temper tantrum, she can hear him bumping the wall heading back to her room, not doubt aiming to add fuel to the fire. He is gone only moments, but it is plenty of time for Jerica to call him every weird name she can think of in his absence under her breath. She's just about to start to yell asking him where he went but after she gets the first word out, he reappears. Upon his return, with the same disturbing look on his face, he hands Jerica a white envelope with her name on it and a single rose. The rose hits the floor because she only snatches the envelop. "What is this a plane ticket back to Texas?" Opening the envelope slowly without taking her eyes from the smudged face man, Jerica pulls out a card.

Her initial thought was how strange it is to have mail and her facial expression showed it. From the smile dropping from grandpa's face to the evil pout that replaced it, Jerica allowed her eyes to drop from his. "That face is uglier than the first one, just so you'd know." Jerica is aiming to hurt his feelings. Looking down at the card her eyes are fixed on its sights. The beauty of the card is annoying but catches her by surprise. On the front of the card, there are black and gold flowers, spiral patterned lines artistically placed winding around the flowers and words. On the outside the card reads. Feel better soon. On the inside of the card is bare on one side. On the other side a handwritten note that says:

My Dearest Jerica,

I apologize for not being at your side when you awoke.

Please forgive me. I had to run to the store to pick up a few items. I want to speak with you in depth about our future upon my return.

Can't wait to see you, bye for now.

Jonathan Slack

Jerica is looking at the letter with dismay. Feeling out of breath and at the same time thinking to herself, "how delusional". She can feel the outburst bubbling in her guts and stomach. The nasty words are on the tip of her tongue. She cannot hold back her hysteria.

She flicks the card across the room and starts losing control. First starting in an even tone. "How delusional? What does he mean by our future?" First turning up her attitude and then her tone, her eyes rolling in the back of her head. "How is this supposed to work? Does he expect me to just be compliant? I remember him referring to me as wife and Michael as son. Yeah, this is what I saw my life as the foolery of being, what? Kidnapping? Imprisoned?" Now, Jerica is full on screaming stressing every word. "Whose clothes am I wearing? Where are the children? What happened to their mother?" Mr. Grumpy says nothing only stares at her as she questions the logistics of her situation. This makes her feel even more infuriated. "Get out! Get out! Get out!" Jonathan enters the room frowning. His face is still very weary. Robert pushes passed him.

He spoke.

CHAPTER 8 : WHAT HAPPENED

"Their mother was presumed dead from the accident you caused and left the scene of as far as I know. Michael is attending class while Sapphire is currently down for a nap, that's why Father was able to come by and look in on you. The clothes you have on were bought especially for you. I would like for you to be compliant because my intention is to provide you with abundant options opposite the life you have been living, however, I understand if you don't want to be compliant. If you choose to be noncompliant, you must understand the consequences of your actions may not only affect you but will more than likely have some effects on the children. Did I forget anything?" Jerica answers with a low but direct and rather intimidating voice. "How is this supposed to work?" Barely meeting his gaze because although he looks both sad and tired today, he seems to be more in control. He speaks with more authority rather than like a person set out to instill fear. Jonathan's facial features change positions once again. His body physically sunken. He looks even more tired than before. "I wanted to speak to you regarding your future, but you have screwed up my mood. Hopefully I can stomach you later so I would appreciate if we could have this talk after dinner."

Hearing the mess that just happened between Jonathan and Jerica is the reason Robert's extremely less than attractive self comes. He rests in the doorway of the room Jerica is in. He stands there with his wrists together and fingers intertwined while his feet are gapped apart as if his son needs security from little ole Jerica. After a few seconds of Jonathan standing and saying nothing else, he turns and walked from the room. His father is slow and calculated exits the room behind him. The already annoying old man is shaking his head as if he's disappointed. "I don't believe I am the one that deserves the head shake. What about you weirdos?" For several moments after they leave, she stares at the closed door behind them wondering what is happening.

Everyone is gone, Jerica puts in a movie called The Twilight Collection. Before she knew it, she is off into the world of mysteries, better known as her dreams. This one is yet again the same uncomfortable, repetitive scene of the accident. Flashes of light, baby crying, and blurred vision. All she feels is the continued pain that's not from her bruised body. She feels the pains of someone hurting. Despite the turmoil an unspeakable calm comes over her suddenly.

The torturous scene she sees is of the damaged cars. Jerica sees herself begin to approach them cautiously. As she moves closer the cars are getting further and further away. Panic, uncertainty and anxiety all leaves her body. She focuses her eyes she sees a tall golden skinned man crying in mourning and because Jerica can't see why he is crying nothing's making sense. At the scene of the accident there were no men present. Still walking towards the abandoned cars, they seem to have stopped retracting. The man is getting more into her view. Its him, Jonathan, but what does he have to cry about? His angry face slowly raises up to meet her gaze. The expression he has on his face is haunted and heavy. When their eyes lock, in an instance

Jerica is transported into Jonathan's sadness and now knows who was creating a sad start to her dream. He is reaching out to her. Robert appears out of nowhere with a sign. The sign reads "He him." Jonathan is still reaching for Jerica. She is disgusted by the action because she doesn't want to feel him touch her. Bile arises in Jerica's throat and she begins to gasp for hair. Choking and drowning she has no choice but to fight to wake up.

Jerica jumps awake. "What is wrong with me? How did I know I was dreaming again?" She searches the room quickly for someone that may have felt the need to continue the weirdness and watch her sleep. No one is in the room with her this time. She can feel an instant relief come over her. The room is slightly lit by the movie screen that shows the three main characters in The Twilight Collection on the screen saver. During her search around the room she notices there are clothes laid out, presumably, for her on the foot of her bed. As her eyes are drawn towards the articles of clothing, she also notices her leg where her restraint was. Finally, she is free to move about in the room. At the time of her previous assessment of the room Jerica didn't notice the door between the chair and the entertainment set. It's a bathroom. The bathroom door is open, and the shower is on.

Dangling her feet from the side of the bed it's so tall her feet doesn't reach the floor. Jerica is straining to touch the floor. By her surprise she doesn't ache as bad as she was before. Which seems strange. She stretches her body as she walks towards the open door. Walking into the steamy bathroom and it's very spacious. The walls are yellow but the area where the shower is, is very dark. Black even. Straight ahead from the doorway is the shower, to the left there is a separate tub and to the right is a black marble vanity and toilet separated by the shower walls. She stepped into the shower without hesitation and is easily relaxed by the hot running water. Focusing first on just standing under the hot water. The water is baptizing her from her conscious to both her soul and the soles of her feet. "There is no guilt in standing here and feeling this good." She says out loud to convince herself she is not in any hurry. Jerica closes her eyes and imagines the time she was in the shower at the apartments in her old hood. Deitrick and Shawn beat on the window too hard and her dad came bursting in the bathroom. Jerica screamed from both events. She giggled out loud and whispered "Dad" shaking her head and smiling at the same time. Her dad that day beat both Shawn and Deitrick until they got enough sense to leave Jerica alone. She washed her neck remembering the first time Jeremy kissed her there. As the bath sponge crossed her shoulder she softly whispered, "I really hate shots." The rest of her shower was full of slow caresses and smiles as every place on her body has memories.

After her hot shower, Jerica is still in no rush. Filling her time with pampering herself giving some much-needed attention to every curve. Taking the same path of caress from her shower, Jerica moisturizes every area of her body continues to stretch her muscles. Her clothes that was laid out for her is the taste of the stylish, not her own. She is wearing a gold, loose fitting, silk dress with black buttons from neck to bottom, stops a few inches from her knee where the dress stops lying near the dress. This adds a quiet class to the ensemble. There was a thin gold necklace and bracelet set. Flat black shoes made of cloth with a silk covering and gold soles, accompanied to finish the look. She knows everything she has on is expensive and she would have never had anything like this had she chosen something for herself using her own funds. Last of her pampering seems to be the most expressive thing a woman can own. A nice full head of amazing hair. Her nice clean hair gives her more than enough reason to stand in the mirror and slowly get some of her confidence back. Jerica takes full advantage of not being tied to the bed. The panicked and evil feelings she's had since her arrival is slowing leaving. "It's only been four days and the only thing that has changed is the amount of light in the room. None of this madness is normal." She hates to have to remind herself of the horror she has endured. A feeling of sadness returns slightly when she remembers the home at her college she hasn't and probably will never make it to. Her thoughts turn to her mother and sister and the relaxation she felt in the shower has dissipated.

Jerica walks into the room quietly and just take a survey of what the atmosphere is like in the room Jonathan is grabbing an item from the counter and setting them on the table. Robert and Michael are making themselves comfortable while baby girl is already in a highchair. Jerica finds her place and sits down at the table. Everyone is star struck as they all stare at her. Michael, Sapphire, Jonathan and his father, all eyes on her. "Well this is uncomfortable." Jerica decides to say under her breath. The second first thing that comes to her mind regards the kitchen. The dining layout mimics a fancy restaurant. Everything is clean and clear. Granite and stainless steel but mostly stainless steel. It's beautiful. Trying to be subtle Jerica's eyes continuously undress the room. Quickly thinking how much fun it would be to cook in something this nice. Jonathan on the other hand doesn't seem to be rich either. The layout of his home is undoubtedly nice and tasteful, but his personal appearance and the looks of his father is nothing more than borderline basic. Basically, borderline basic. The lumberman jack looks they both seem to stick with is nothing like the silk goddess they turned Jerica into.

Looking around the table after moments of being in her own head and passing judgement. At this moment in Jerica's mind, she cannot help but think of how wrong this is. Her appearance doesn't take away from the heaviness she feels in the pit of her stomach. Chained to a bed when she woke up this morning, but now, she's sitting here dressed in what she calls the best linings she will ever wear. Jerica is hungry and that is the reason she is out of the room. She decides to turn her attitude down and turn her attention to her meal.

The plated dinner in front of her contains whole kernel corn, thin cut T-bone steak and a loaded baked potato with chives, butter, pepper, bacon bits, sour cream and cheese all in metal cups gathered beside her plate. There is a small side salad on the left side of the plated dinner. Instead of the hard liquor she prefers, her mean is served with a glass of sparkling water. Looks like someone spent a lot of time on this food. Looks can be deceiving but that is probably untrue. There is likely a chef somewhere hidden who deserves all the credit. Looking up from her plate, Jerica looks around the table waiting for someone to speak to make things less awkward.

Jonathan is still staring at her. As a matter of fact, the only one who has lost interest in what she looks like is Sapphire. Jonathan and Michael speak in unison, "You are very beautiful." With her lips slightly parted, Jerica cannot believe their reaction to her appearance when this situation is so disturbing. She can't help but hold on to the misery that is still not clear as to what is really happening right now. Embarrassed and unsure what to do, she looks back down at her plate. Under the table she is twiddling her fingers. Although her eyes found a comfortable place to rest the muscles in her cheek bones did her no favors. She could not control her facial expression. She tried. "Jerica, is something wrong with your meal? If so, I can make you something else to eat." Jonathan is sincere when he asked. With all of the fuss over her, Jerica lost all of her confidence and sense of anger. This is every woman's dream, to have a good-looking man who cooks, a beautiful little girl who has the sweetest face and a handsome son who has compassion and love in his heart surrounding her. Googly eyed at her. Telling her she is beautiful. But her conscience will not allow her to go along with this charade. She can't pretend. "I want to be happy." She said the words before she knew what was happening. "Jonathan, what is this." tears streaming down Jerica's face. "Can we have this conversation now?" Jonathan sighed and nodded in the direction of his father who then takes Sapphire and Michael to the next room.

CHAPTER 9 : CHANGE OF SCENERY

"Let's start with the basics." Jonathan speaks in a clear, unhurried, slightly direct but even tone. "My name is Jonathan Darcel Slack. I teach English Literature at Amir University, which is an online college, which means I work out of my home office. The man you see that will not speak is my father. His name is Robert Paul Slack. He lives here with us. You are my wife. At home, your name can still be Jerica Stevenson but on paper your name is now Jewell Slack and our children are Robert Darcel Slack and baby Star Nicole Slack. I want you to be comfortable. Do you understand?" He pauses for a response but doesn't get one. "I want this to be a peaceful solution to both of our problems. Everyday problems that we fight against mostly alone we will combat together. We are each other's solution." Her eyes are filled with tears that won't fall.

Jerica says nothing, only shakes her head as if to shake the thoughts away while her tears slowly build. "This is not to hurt you; this is to give you an out from the life you had. You can change the things that wasn't working in your favor and enhance those qualities that are working." Jerica starts to shake her head harder and now sobbing as quietly as she can while he continues. "I want you to learn how to put your fear to work. Use it as a gain and stop fighting to hide it. Fearing what naturally is, is not a solution but a Band-Aid. I can help you put fear in its place. I want to show you my F.E.A.R. and you can learn to use that to your advantage as well." Looking up at him in disgust once again as he tells her what seems to be the dark dumb mess swirling around in his head. Back and forth Jerica starts shaking away how normal he is trying to make this all sound.

"So, at this point, you have no idea what life

I've had, you just assume I need a change of scenery. I am to depend totally on you to give me a new life. I didn't ask you for any of this!" Jerica is speaking with her head turned down. Slowly raising her head towards him. She cannot look at him, only towards his general direction. He knows it too. "Jerica look at me." Jonathan's looks turn cold. He started spilling his thoughts as fast as he could. Almost as if they were rehearsed. "You knocked on my door, spilling your soul trying to get help for that woman and her kids. I see you as a caring and thoughtful person. Even in the state you were in I seen how beautiful you are. I wanted to help you. The focus was always you, never what your issues are or what they were or were not. I will give you all the love and attention you need. I'm capable of that. I've done it before. I will never leave you. Who will ever opt to have the opposite of any of these things? I know this is crazy and I know this will take some time to adjust to for both of us. My last wife died a few months ago and we never had children, so I am starting over, with you and the kids. You may not understand it but talk to me, ask what you want. This is your chance for dialogue."

He started to unbuckle his plaid shirt as if he has something that is making him hot and annoyed. At this moment she looked away from him turning her entire body in her chair to face a different direction. Jonathan is still staring at Jerica and she can still feel it. She stares down at her untouched plate and picks up her fork. He continues to speak after a short pause, "I know you want to have children and I know you are unmarried and unattached." Listening to these words, she drops her fork and grips her chest in agony. Sobbing uncontrollably while straining to allow herself to comprehend Jonathan's attempt at making the puzzle pieces fit together for her. Jerica cannot fix her face long enough to respond. Still crying she pleads, "Not this way, you have taken away my choices. Today in the world you do not have to be a good-looking man, why couldn't you just find love, adopt children, become a foster father? There are ways to feed your obsession to help people! There are people who want that type of help. They yearn for it. This way is wrong." Jerica questioned further. The story for her just doesn't add up. She is upset and not at ease by any means despite all the pretty words Jonathan has spat at her. "You don't get it; I don't care what you want or what you have cooked up in your head. I want you to do the right thing and help me in ways I can benefit from and that's to help me get home to my sister and mother." There's a short pause just enough time for her to wipe her nose on the provided napkin. She starts again, "you shouldn't want a miserable household. This is kidnap, or don't you care?"

Jonathan is content with his decision to have Jerica be his wife and he knows he has to be patient with her, and the idea is not so easy to comprehend. "This is hard, I know, but my gut tells me we can do this. Keep the hurt in our lives away by finding something to replace those things with each other. I mean what do you want from life?" He pauses once again for her response. "If you are interested in me, why are you dead set on going about love like this? Why do I have to be away from my family to do this? Why couldn't your approach be keeping in contact with me. Keeping me close and developing a real relationship with me while I am still living my own life?" Jerica decided to keep the questions coming. "This is normal for you? Isn't it? This is how you got your last wife? Isn't it?"

As she takes a breath, Jonathan takes the opportunity to continue to fill in the blanks for her. "I needed time to get information. You were unconscious for so long I had no choice but to go ahead and get it done." She tries to interrupt him. "None of this is making sense, get what done?" He doesn't stop what he is saying to reply to her rudeness. "I needed to make sure you would get better I just couldn't wait. I took the liberty to change your identity so that you can start life over once you were back to your original state of mind. In time we will add your family to the loop and help them understand. We have to show a united front and make sure your life is better with me. You have to be willing to give me a chance, Jerica."

Jonathan is relaxing with his back against his chair, because this is beginning to be a conversation. All dramatics and egos aside. Moving in the right direction. Still speaking in a controlled voice, Jonathan proceeds carefully because he knows this can easily turn left no matter how well he thinks he is doing, Jerica is still crying and gripping her chest so he tries to appeal to her life goals and dreams he is sure a new identity can assist with. "Do you want to start a business, go to school?" Jerica continues to look straight. "No, I want to go home!" She shouts to his surprise. "I can help give you the life you want, we just need to do it together. I found out you were enrolling into college in Chicago." Jerica's attitude and discomfort are growing. "So! You think you know me, but you truly have no idea who I am. I want to go home!" Jonathan takes a step that may cost him an eye. Moving closer to Jerica, Jonathan continues to spill his thoughts, but she is not responding to his point of view anymore. Jonathan avoids addressing Jerica's pain thinking maybe she will come around. When his pretty words don't work anymore, he tries a different approach.

Aggression. He figured he'd give her the meat and potatoes of this meal because she hasn't eaten what's on her plate. "I want you. Your entire life has been wiped away. There is nothing for you to return to. You should get used to being here. We can live in misery or you can accept your reality which is designed to erase all F.E.A.R. and make the best of it. You will never escape. You will raise these children and you will live a full life. With my help. Once the time is right, we will find your family and they can come too." Feeling the anger pouring from his pores and not liking the tone he is taking with her, Jerica looks Jonathan squarely in the eyes and tells him without a crack in her voice, "Your anger does not scare me. I will leave here, I will be taking the children and finding their real family and I will return to mines." Stressing the word "will" every time it's said she is making herself crystal clear to Jonathan.

Jerica was right to think Jonathan was upset. "You women. All colors, white, black, purple women, you are all the same. You don't even pretend to be the sweet perfect black woman that I know you are. Instead want me to believe you are just the same as the rest of your ungrateful, cock grabbing, can't let go of their pride species. You all are always trying to find something wrong. You have someone willing to grab a hold of you with no intentions on letting you go, and you want to run. That is why you are treated the way that you are in society." Jonathan storms back to his side of the table pacing the floor. Knocking his chair over rushing back over to Jerica's side, he throws her plate of food to the floor and whisper in her ear, "remember this address, you will be back, no one's looking for you." Unbothered by his anger, Jerica starts up again. "Oh, let's forget that I've been kidnapped, let's forget you are trying to brainwash everyone in this situation to think we are one big happy family. You want me to play maid and mommy. You are as dumb as you look if you think for a second that I am going to let you make me feel like I am the one out of my mind here." Jerica is up out of her seat now. She wipes the tears from her face continuing to yell. "How dare you compare me to women you know; you know nothing about me. How dare you turn angry towards me. Flipping over chairs will not make me stay here.

You have shown me nothing but pure craziness! Tying me up, trying to take away from who I am. You have sat at this table and spewed your ugly judgmental words at me. Babbling on and on about fear and such! You will not destroy me, I am leaving. Bring me the children", she screams as loud as she can to make her request clear.

Back and forth they scream and yell as Jerica stands her ground and Jonathan paces the floor. Jerica screams again. Even louder this time, as if he didn't hear her the first time. "You're an insane coward, bring me the children!" Jerica's eyes are bloodshot red. "No!" Jonathan tells her, "go, run, go make a life for yourself or whatever it is you want to do. If you are successful, then I have failed, and I will be all too willing to give you the children." He stops pacing the floor. At this point both children and Robert stand in the doorway that opens to the kitchen.

"You call it running. I call it getting back to my own life. And for the children, I will do the right thing." One last look into Jonathan's eyes, then Jerica turns to the children and Robert. Robert is staring back at her with even more angry eyes than normal and both kids are looking surprised and clueless. Jerica walks out of the door.

CHAPTER 10 : BYE

Jerica took notice at the doorknob on the front door as she slammed it shut. The gold knob is shedding its topcoat of paint no doubt due to the harsh weather. The door itself was a bronze color stained with some kind of paint that glittered. Jerica couldn't help but associate the mesmerizing glitter to the children's book Hansel and Gretel. "Oh, get over it!" Jerica rolled her eyes at herself and how her short attention span took over. Snapping out of the trans from the dazzling door, Jerica turns toward the street. She puts one foot in front of the other setting out to leave. No money and no one to call, Jerica is literally coasting in no man's water in the wrong direction up the creek without a paddle. She doesn't even know what day it is but she is determined to live a full life in control and not die a captivity. Although to some, the proposition made by Jonathan would sound like heaven, to someone as giving, hardworking and loyal as Jerica is, this whole thing sounds like a torturous nightmare. The person that would prey on the weak, desperate, incapacitated and powerless soul is just not a good person. Freedom is not something a person should negotiate. "True freedom is acting, thinking and speaking uninfluenced and unjudged. He tried to make it sound so normal to the complete opposite." Jerica cannot grab a hold of Jonathan's nerve or concept.

"What would make a person lie and scheme to take something that a normal person is designed to willingly and freely give. Love, affection, and success are life goals for most women, but we crave a person to share them with." Talking her thoughts out loud doesn't make her feel any better. "Why are men so clueless and domineering?" As sure as the words fall from her lips, she realizes that no one is there to answer her question when she turns toward the empty street. Being outside is a gift so she breathes deeply her first whiff of fresh air she'd had since the horrible night she fell on the steps of this maniac. Jerica pauses to exhale but quickly collected herself before she is met with the insane giant who lives in this house. The long walk away from the door to the curb gave Jerica so much more confidence. Her subconscious is using the pain in the pit of her stomach to fuel each step. She turned to peer at the window and caught a glimpse of the shadows. The image was too large to be anyone she'd already met in the house. Both Jonathan and Robert were fairly fit men. As she watched the window, the image split in half heading two different directions. Her mind instantly concluded Robert was consoling Jonathan. Jerica was against letting her life of hardship and struggle give an impression that she was even considering compliance. If this was a man and wife situation, she would not hesitate stepping back into the crazy lady mode. Jerica turned and began proceeding to the path toward "Operation: Get Out". "I will not waste the opportunity the heavens have given me." Jerica pauses and looks towards the light open sky, "God you did not have to let me walk out of this house, but you did and I thank you."

The curb to her is a symbol that holds a great deal of power. Looking down at the curb, "I made it and I am free. I am not a part of this badly made horror movie anymore." She repeated the mantra to herself for power and strength about 3 more times. "Looking forwards and not behind." Jerica continues to speak life, power and focus into herself.

First looking left and then right, Jerica sets out to complete step one towards the plan for getting free. "First stop, the police station. Well the actual first stop is finding the police station." Tears travel from her eyes then rolling down her face because now Jerica knows more and better that she has no clue as to where she is or where she is going. Jerica wipes her tears and continues thinking out loud in a muffled voice. "I made it and I am free. I am not a part of this badly made horror movie anymore." Clearer and more confidence is present in her voice every time she says it. "Looking forwards and not behind."

Jerica is wandering around in the middle of the street. "I've made it to the street, now what Jerica." She's thinking out loud again. It's nearing six in the evening and the sun is setting nicely. Looking down the street to the left, she sees more houses. Looking to her right, there are houses but farther off she sees what seems to be the corner store lights. She heads towards the lights slightly afraid and skeptical. "What choice do I have!" she exclaims stomping her foot and rolling her eyes at herself. "Looking forwards and not behind."

Not knowing where she is or where the police station is, she walks until she is face to face with the corner store. It turns out to be a gas station. On the front door there was no presence of a hanging doorbell, the place looks kind of deserted. The gas station looks functional but a bit slow for this time of night. No one in immediate sights so Jerica moves around the store looking for someone to help her. Passing the nuts on the first endcap, there was no one down either aisle. Also passing the endcap full of chargers with on one in sights or recognizable movements. Jerica decided she was still hungry, and she was going to get her an energy drink if no one was coming out to help her. "I know what's going on, the cashier is off have relations no doubt with her boyfriend that isn't supposed to be here in the first place." She's thinking out loud again. Jerica makes it to the freezer section as she's rambling on and on about inappropriate things when the presence of a person startles the booboo right out of her.

Long dark hair covered with an all-black Razorbacks hat is kneeled in the back of the store. The cashier wears a black shirt that reads Princess Sassy on the back. As she turns slightly to the side to grab more cans to restock, she reveals her gray eyes covered with full lashes and heavy makeup. She is hungrily chewing gum as if she won't give up trying to squeeze more flavor out of it. The cashier is stocking the freezer with adult beverages. Most of these drinks Jerica never even heard of as she decides to glance around from a distance before making the young lady aware of her presence. She approaches the lady calling out to her before she's standing too closely, careful so she doesn't startle the cashier. "Hello." Somehow it seems she already knew Jerica was in the store so once Jerica started to speak, she was already gathering herself to her feet. Their gazes meet as the cashier stops what she is doing to focus on what Jerica need. The cashier stands up and walks in her direction before any other words are spoken. Jerica is able to read her name tag that says "hi my name is Alisha" written in blue ink on an all-white card.

"Hey, let me know if you need help finding anything." Alisha says while walking passed Jerica and stopping to fix items on the shelf. "Hi there, I don't need to purchase anything, but can I ask you for directions?" her Jerica asked hopeful Jonathan hadn't worked some kind of contact and got to the store clerk before she did. "Yeah where to?" Alisha says as she is smiling as big as possible. "The police station. I'm not from around here, if any way possible could you write the directions down?" Jerica gives off the sweet persona Alisha is giving off. "Yeah sure come, follow me to the front." Alisha is moving quickly to the front and behind the counter.

The young lady gives Jerica play by play directions written on the back of a blank receipt on how to get to the police station. The store looks small on the outside but very spacious on the inside. Every customer that walks through the door looks Jerica in the eyes making her very nervous. She can't decide whether or not the feelings she has is from paranoia or are these people sent by Jonathan. She thinks to herself wondering if everyone knows what is happening. Before she knows it, Alisha is done explaining and handing her the map.

Jerica set out on her journey to find the police station. When Alisha explained how to get there, the part Jerica heard, she made it so simple that Jerica felt as if it was a skip, hop and a jump away. What wasn't taken into consideration was the fact that she was walking and not driving in a car. Walking along the trail out of the housing complex, there are many people that look like there is no home for them to go to. Women and a few men. The atmosphere of this part of the community seems to be set apart from everywhere else. It's the hood on one side but on the other hand it's strange. Jerica was not scared of these people because where she's from there are many houses like this. They call them shotgun houses. Just means they houses has no personality. You can see the back door from the front door. The people who live there gives the houses its reputations. People with no purpose but to hang out. Just cheap affordable housing to stay close to the goings on in the community they live in. Although, this feels colder and more distant from reality, it looks the same.

As she moved on through the community, she was able to see the bright side of things. The houses on the outside were ran down but fully functional as people stood out in the yard or sitting on the porch. She encountered people who waved at her. There was even one man who tried to come on to her. He asked, "Hey beautiful, where are you headed." Jerica is ignoring him. "Can I come walk with you." Jerica with a little attitude in her voice told the man, "I'm headed to the police station, still want to come?" Jerica raises an eyebrow. She watched him throw up both hands and gave a small smile. Jerica never even stopped walking. She gave a forced angry half smile back, an eyebrow still raised. To her, this exchange of words was the first positive interaction with a male that she has encountered as far as she can remember. Thinking to herself maybe Arkansas isn't filled with crazy people.

Jerica is feeling herself relax as she walks. Mind moving a million miles an hour. Remembering she hasn't eaten anything; she is very hungry. She isn't weak but her stomach is making it very clear it is time to eat. "It's a shame I didn't eat when I had the chance." This has been the first time Jerica has thought about food, other than as a distraction, since she woke up this morning. Speaking her thoughts out loud as she often tends to do Jerica says to herself, "if Jonathan had not thrown my food on the floor, maybe I would have taken my plate, then again he may have poisoned it to keep me from asking questions or maybe to even force me to be compliant." The thought makes Jerica angry again and she begins to walk faster and faster. "There's nothing more than stinking assumptions. There is nothing clear here."

Finally making it far enough into the city that she can see something other than grass, trees and weathered fences, Jerica runs into a grocery store called The Market Place. Ducking inside to use the restroom, she can't help but see food and think about how truly hungry she is. After finding the restroom and drinking some water from the fountain, Jerica can't help but wonder how and when she will get the chance to eat. It's time she tries her hand at shoplifting." How?" she says out loud as she weighs her options. There is no particular plan and she is literally scared out of her mind. "Looking forwards and not behind." She says under her breath to find more of the decision-making strength she was able to channel before. Rolling her eyes towards the heavens Jerica repeats it a few more times.

She is still wearing the dress that was hand-picked out for her by her pretend husband and the expensive shiny shoes also. Looking down at herself she feels no one will ever attempt to suggest she has the need to steal anything. Jerica walked down the can good aisle. "I could hold a can between my legs." As the words flow from her lips in a whisper Jerica knows there will not be an easy way to make it to the front door without looking suspicious. Down the bread aisle there are a few more choices. She runs her hands down the shelf full of little debbies. The boxes are too hard and square to make for an easy grab. Jerica sets eyes on the rolls. The dress is flowy and loose fitting enough that Jerica is able to hide a pack of Hawaiian rolls at the flat of her back. "Yes, that's exactly what I'll do."

There are not many people in the store at the time she decides to make her move. Jerica was able to access where the cameras are and find a place down the coffee aisle where she can execute this unplanned event. Dropping to one knee she kneels down close to an aisle display. The large cardboard coffee display is the ideal spot. She slips the package under the front of her dress. Slowly standing up she is pushing the loaf from her front to her back. "Too easy to be that easy."

Her heart is beating fast the entire time. The loud talking and playful horse playing the cashiers are doing keeps her attention focused on not getting caught because at any time someone could come down the aisle. The rim of her panties safely secures the entire loaf at the small of her back. Once the bread is positioned, she is now able to push her stomach out as far as it will go to add an extra security. Her body now fills up the dress, which keeps the bread in place, but she still tugs on her panties as she walks. Paranoia sets in when her silk panties begin to shift. Everything is in place, but Jerica has to try very hard to convince herself that's true.

Jerica walks up the next aisle where the condiments are and stops at the pickles to continue to adjust herself. Pulling her panties up over the package helps her be able to walk right out of the store without raising an eyebrow in her direction. Finally, she is able to breathe. She makes sure to walk out and make eye contact with every single person. Giving them the bubbly personality, she had before tragedy struck. Everyone gives her back the energy she gives them. There is an unfamiliar woman that is overly pleasant and greets Jerica back briefly. The woman is sweet as she asks Jerica how is she doing and acknowledges Jerica's attire. The disturbance the woman causes trying to be too nice doesn't help Jerica's mood at all.

Jerica walks towards the parking lot as she hurriedly tells the woman thank you and wish her a wonderful day. Between a few cars she creates a window of opportunity to devour the meal she just scored. Before deciding the perfect time to take out the bread, Jerica surveys the entrance to the parking lot to see if there were cars pulling in. Next, she looks behind her at the entrance to make sure no one is exiting. All while using the cars as a cover the bread is out without being smashed.

Walking and eating her bread Jerica have no shame. Her stomach has been growling for the last hour. This is a good day, the wind is slightly blowing, but not enough for Jerica to be cold.

She begins dialogue out loud speaking only with herself to take her mind off of her surroundings and current situation. Some of the passing cars are stopping trying to get Jerica to get inside the car but she can't trust anyone in this town.

"The bigger picture, Jerica is that I, I mean you, which is also I, will finally be able to get home. I know my family must be worried sick. I have to find the family of those poor children." As she walks and tries to keep herself going, Jerica realizes there is not much to go home to. It also crosses her mind that she doesn't even know what will happen at the police station. Continuing her conversation, "Really, what am I doing? Who knows what those children was involved in before making here? As far as I know neither child has been injured. I'm sure the police will be able to break Michael's silence enough to decide what's best for him and his sister. That is not my job. I've never taken care of any children before. I don't know what's best for them." Jerica ignores a car passing by asking her if she needs someone to talk to. The thoughts don't stop coming. They are convicting in a way but also not wanting to get too much involved. She is at the point now that she's unsure of her next move, which starts to weigh heavy on her.

There is a sign that indicates turning left at the stop light and in doing so you are on the correct path to the police station. From the looks of the image on the sign, the station is more like a house. The road seems never ending but she forges forward speaking to herself and finishing off the bread.

CHAPTER 11 : 5 MONTHS

Jerica made it to her destination without incident. More of the same borderline harassment from civilians was to be expected anyway. Jerica approaches a brick building that looks like it could have been a house for a very large family once upon a time. "I'm sure there's no cells in this precinct." Jerica mouthed as she climbed the 4 stairs leading to the front door. The police station inside is very small. Mountains of paperwork, cabinets, lockers, and small desk makes the place look cluttered. Beyond the receptionist desk are many heads without bodies. Looks weird, but it's plain to see everyone is working extremely hard as they're glued to their desk. When she walked through the door there is a glass wall straight ahead.

Hard at work, everyone busies themselves. She is immediately met by one male cop and a female cop that can barely be seen from the huge computer screens. The lady cop starts to speak first without doubt by protocol because these days everyone is a victim. "Hello, how may I help you?" The lady cop has a mousey but raspy voice. She probably smokes cigarettes. "Hey there, I would like to make a police report." Jerica is confident as she draws back her shoulders and steady her hands. "Sure, ma'am, what's your name?" As if the million-dollar question has been asked, Jerica answers with a twist to her lips. "My name is Jerica Stevenson and my identity has been stolen." The officer begins her long line of questions. Jerica answers carefully because first things first, she has to see how truthful Jonathan has been with her. It's hard to hear or even comprehend what the lady officer is saying with the bullet proof glass between them. Still, she answers each question with her sweetest attitude.

In the middle of Jerica's victory, she has to hide her annoyance when a man walks in the police station asking for the lost and found. Jerica, for a second, thinks she may have saw him in the grocery store but doesn't dwell on the thought. He is talking a little too loudly. Because they both cannot stand there talking and understand clearly what each officer is saying, the nice police lady tells Jerica to come through the door and stand to the right of it. Jerica walks through the door and is instructed to sit down in a wooden chair. Jerica is sitting too closely to the first desk through the door. The lady police introduced herself as Officer Robins and continued with her line of questioning. Never missing a beat, she still is able to notice the bustle among the cliques in the station.

Officer Robin's eyes are darting from the computer and then around the four corners of the room behind her. The man that was looking for lost and found has now entered in the same door Jerica did and their eyes meet. Jerica gets the shivers which takes the attention from the stranger and places it on herself. Officer Robins notices, "are you ok Ms. Stevenson?" She asked with genuine concern. "Yes, everything is just fine. Have you found anything in your system yet?" Jerica tries to divert the conversation back to the problem at hand. "It will take a while to find the information as I will be conducting a thorough search. The database here in this precinct will only reach so far through the surrounding counties. Searches outside of the state will definitely have to be done out of this office. The information you provided has to be turned over to the proper investigators and once we have information, we can reach out to you. Do you have a phone number for me us reach out to you when we've found something?" Jerica turns her attention to her moisturized hands trying to fight back her tears afraid to answer. "I didn't think..." Jerica stops mid-sentence.

Concrete walls and barely carpeted floors give a very cold ambiance to the room. None of this is helping Jerica's mood. She starts to look around the room for inspiration to what her next move is going to be. Also trying not to directly look into the officer's eyes, Jerica finds out by the calendar blocks on Officer Robin's desk the date is September 20, 2017. First panic and then worry settles in. The last date she can remember is the day she left for her trip which was April 4, 2017. Confusion then turns to anger; anger turns to anxiety and shortly after Jerica is back to being panicked. "Is today really September 20, 2017?" Her voice is small but each word is pronounced perfectly. "Oh no, today is actually the 21st, we rotate desk here, guess no one has been sitting here to change it." The officer offers a clueless explanation with a smile on her face. With all of the feelings that rush over Jerica in an instant she begins to speak "I'm drowning, I can't breathe!" Gripping her chest Jerica is reaching out to grab ahold of the officer but darkness takes over her mind. She starts falling to the floor as she loses control of her arms and legs. Jerica can hear Officer Robins shouting numbers and then her eyes are closed.

"How can this be, I have been missing for 5 months" she recites this over and over again as the paramedics starts an intravenous therapy and blood pressure cuff. She tells the officer her name is Jerica Stevenson and she has been missing since her car accident. Jerica is irate and distraught trying to explain what is happening, but no one seems to be listening only working.

"Ma'am we need you to calm down, we think you had a seizure. Please stay still." One of the boys in an over washed t shirt underneath his paramedic uniform shirt. "No, can you hear me? I need your help." Jerica is ignored as the paramedics continue to try to calm her. Shaking her head and trying to persuade at least one of the three men to listen to her she hasn't stopped talking yet. Darkness begins to overtake her once again. Her body is limp, but her mind and ears are still alert.

"Jerica!!! Can you hear me?? Mom and dad say you are better off with us!" Before she can respond to her sister's commands, she hears voices speaking over her. Fluttering her eyes open as they protest to comply, Jerica tries opening her mouth, but no words are forming. She begins to try to move her hand towards the tubes in her nose, but nothing. Jerica lays there a few moments without stressing while giving her body time to wake up. She can hear them. Next to her hospital bed, the officer is explaining how they cannot find a Jerica Stevenson in the local or national database. "Jerica gives a social security number that comes up to be a person that has been deceased for over ten years. No school records, no doctor visits, no debt, nothing!" The doctor and nurses are continuing to talk while Jerica can feel them moving around the room and her bedside. The machines are beeping all around her. She still cannot move. "I hear you!" she is screaming but no one can hear her because she isn't fully conscious yet again. Again, Jerica begin to freak out. "She has to be having a nightmare." Jonathan is shouting. The bed is shaking, and Jerica is physically being held down.

"She is still out cold; the medication she was given she is allergic to. We didn't find that out until she started to break out in hives. Her face was swelling, and she's been given meds to counteract the toxins. This could be more side effects." Everyone is talking and hustling around the room. "Last time she had this, I thought I'd killed her, could this be a seizure?" Jonathan is out of his mind. "What the hell did you do?" Jonathan sounds mad.

People are talking all around in her head. Jerica hasn't the strength to respond or tell them what she is feeling. All different voices all sounding stressed and confused. "Give her another shot, we cannot let her blood pressure go up to what it was when she came here, she'd die."

Jerica hears another voice she doesn't recognize louder than all the rest. Shortly after she doesn't hear the strange voices anymore there is singing. Jerica hears home in the song that is playing. "God is the joy and the strength of my life; he rules all pain misery and strife. Always to keep me, never to leave me, never ever fall short of his word. We have to fast and pray, stay in the narrow way..." the choir is giving me life this morning. Tears stream down her face as she reflects on the words of the song. Jam-Jam is beside her sleep and resting quietly on her shoulder. Her mom and dad are here engulfed in God's grace. The scenery is perfect. The moment is perfect. "God will never lead you to a place he didn't tell you to go. The bible tells you..." Pastor continues. Underneath all of the scenery and goings on, Jerica hears a small voice saying "Play nice, be smart, plan and get out" she becomes aware of what was said and then she hears "play nice, Jerica, boys are only mean if they like you. That's your power." Once again, she hears it. "Play nice, boys are only mean if they like you. That's your power."

Looking around the church most people have their eyes closed worshiping. She doesn't know who is speaking to her, but she is beginning to get paranoid. Jerica hears the mantra again. Frantic she stands up. Some people have started to pay attention to her including her parents. Her mother's face is sympathetic while her father has a pained look on his face. Neither one of them moved a muscle to embarrass her. "Baby, if it's better for you just stay with us." Her mom is speaking to her I the tone of voice she hasn't used since she was about five. Her family has always been very attentive with her. Not spending much time on the thought but she wonders why they aren't moving or attempting to console her. Jerica knows she is asleep now and she wants to wake up. She takes off running around the church trying to get someone's attention, but no one is acknowledging her. Some are watching but no one is moving. Feeling very panicked she continues to run. Looking everyone in the face calling them by name, wanting to reach out and touch one of them but her arms won't allow it. She looks down and she has a prison ball attached to her left leg and both wrists are bound together and attached to the chain on her leg. Something is pulling her. She began to kick and scream. Pulling her hair and grabbing at the prison ball that has her weighed down in an instant spring awake.

Jerica opens her eyes.

CHAPTER 12 : SENDING ME A MESSAGE

Jerica wakes up with a jerk. She recognizes her surroundings pretty quickly. She is in a place she all but hates on the account it holds only painful memories for her, the hospital. Without looking she hears the slow hum of the machines. She also takes note of the reading on the machines and quickly decipher what she's ok. Jerica knows how to read her vitals shown on their respective monitors because her sister was in the hospital once and one of the doctors who attended to Jameria explained what each machine does. With her father battling cancer well into her high school years, she remembers each machine and the horrors she experienced all too well from those turns of events in her life.

In her room one entire wall is glass. Along the other wall to the left there are a bunch of machines and extra beds. To the right of her bed is lots of plugs and paperwork. Jerica's bed is looking directly towards the less private side of the room. There are people straight ahead outside the glass window watching Jerica. They are watching her closely while talking and writing. To her annoyance her headache gets worse as she looks to the left of her bed and see the doctor holding up a perfectly good wall. Jerica remembers vaguely hearing the doctor say "not another one" as they took her from the ambulance into the hospital. What did he mean by that? The decision was made early on in her transition here that she doesn't like anyone at this hospital. Her bad mood is evident and she's sure of it. Slowing taking her attention away from the doctor there is no chance of changing it.

Jerica is not a dummy by far. Her faint state in and out of consciousness shed some light that the good doctor nor the police have believed her story. Although unfortunately the facts of her circumstances do not give Jerica much to support her gut feelings, she still knows she didn't have a soul on her side who she can get to be straight with her about the details as to why.

There is no one. Whispering out loud, "yeah we will see very soon". She realizes just because she is talking in her head, she sounds like the crazy lady she turned into at Jonathan's house.

As he stands there in his blue collared shirt, black tie and the white coat that has name on it, his vibe is inviting. Dr. Walsh is paying too close attention to Jerica. "What are you looking at, man?" Jerica asked the most obvious question. Not because she wanted to know, rather because she is just angry and rightfully so. Turning away from the likes of her intrusive doctor, she has a surprise on the other side. Jerica then turns to face the other wall and is scared to her bones because "he" is here. Right here beside her bed is Jonathan Slack. Annoyance and anger flood her soul. "Why are you here? The yelling and rudeness continue? Haven't you done enough Mr. Slack?" Jerica doesn't hide her anger from him but she does at least try to keep her voice low. He sits in all his glory not reacting at all. Undoubtedly sensing the tension, Dr. Walsh started his rant and they both anchored back down to their present reality and draws their attention to the all-knowing doctor.

For the first part of his rant Jerica is admiring his features. Dr. Walsh is a black man around fifty years old with dark colored eyes and a salt and pepper goatee. His hair is cut low but his grays still peek through. He is extremely good looking. In respects to his height, Dr. Walsh is a little on the taller side. He towers over Jonathan.

"Hey! Are you listening?" Dr. Walsh is getting a little testy. "Now I am. Go ahead Mr. Snappy." Jerica is embarrassed so she answers with anger. The doctor tells her they had to call her next of kin because they thought she was having an allergic reaction to some medication that was administered. "We didn't have much of a medical record to go off of. Looks like you haven't been seen here before." He clears things up. "You could go home once your discharge papers were read if you are feeling better." He continues to explain. "To let you go so soon is not normal protocol. We should have called White Coats. That company works closely with this hospital to perform a full mental evaluation on patients that have no prior background but are showing irrational signs of mental disturbances. The of the level of outburst and ruckus you caused in both the police station and since you have been at the hospital..." Before Dr. Walsh can continue, "Ruckus? What ruckus? I didn't cause any ruckus. What is this?" she finally yells out as her gaze meets Jonathan's. "Jonathan this is you? You've convinced everyone around you that I am some deranged animal huh?" She turns back to look at the doctor. "What is happening here? You said I could leave." Jerica's eyes dart towards the people behind the glass and then back to Jonathan. She continues as Jonathan stares impassively at her, not bothering to try and comfort, soothe or at least explain himself to her.

"You have been sedated all of three times in the week you have been here." She swivels her head as fast as her neck allows so that she's facing back to the doctor. "The week?" Her attention is gathered and her interest is piqued. Dr. Walsh proceeds and starts to mention how it was her husband who told both the hospital and the police about the tragedy. "Someone could have been hurt. The nurses, the student doctors and myself included." Dr. Walsh pauses to let her continue to gather herself once more. "Jewell, we know about your friend passing away in a car accident which is the real reason for your disorientation and if you can assure this will not happen again, we can make sure to release you and forget this terrible interaction."

With the strangest look on her face, she began to piece together how stupid they think she is. She had to catch herself from throwing a fit of rage while bile arose in her throat. Jerica's breath catches and she reaches for her throat and gives herself a gentle rub starting at her chin. Her choices were either to turn into a Tasmanian devil and start gargling at the mouth all while destroying things in her tantrum or throw up. Jerica chose to throw up. All over her, the doctor, the bed and the floor she lets go of everything she had no idea she ate.

Jerica runs through everything that has happened while everyone is tending to the clean-up.

One. I have been kidnapped. Two. I am now married with two kids. Three. My true identity is not known to anyone that could help me. Four. I have been given drugs to knock me out for now a six-month period. Five. Being fed, clothed and bathed by complete strangers. Six. The dead woman from the car which I am now an accomplice to her disappearance. She looks over at Jonathan while all of the CNA's move about the entire room. He is sitting on his high horse and not responding to anything. Jerica's mind is working a half of a mile a minute. She rests on thoughts of the dream she had when she was unconscious. The fact that her mom and dad were together again. She's snapped out of her line of questioning herself when the machine besides her starts to beep. The good doctor begins to read Jerica's vitals. Jerica realizes she still has a chance.

"Doc, have you drawn my blood and if so, what is my blood type?" Jerica starts out playfully. "Yes, Mrs. Slack, we have drawn your blood and your blood type is o+." Jerica smiles. "And Doc, if I had a sister or mother, you would be able to tell what my true identity by my relation to them, is that correct?" Dr. Walsh's facial expression is puzzled, but he still answers every question even in his confusion, "yes, that is correct. If your mother and sister were to come in, yes, we can perform an analysis for relation." The choice of words the doctor used took Jerica aback. Looking at the good doctor and then sharply at Jonathan, Jerica feels the urge to throw up again but doesn't. Dr. Walsh is looking from Jerica to Jonathan and back to Jerica. "Mr. Slack, may I have a private word with you in the hallway, please?" Jerica watches both men as they exit the room.

As Jonathan and the doctor speak, Jonathan's eyes have not left Jerica. Dr. Walsh has his back to the glass so Jerica cannot see what is being said. The students, nurses and CNA's have all left. Saying nothing when he enters the room, but Jerica notices his eyes are even more tired looking than before. "I cannot be the one stressing you out." Jerica begins in on Jonathan. "What is it going to be Jerica? Are you going to come home and fulfill your motherly duties because I am very tired of pulling all of this weight by myself? Or are you going to continue to embarrass us both keeping up this act as if I did not tell you what you were up against." Jonathan is serious. "How am I supposed to answer that? Why do you insist on keeping me here instead of just letting me go home? Is this what a good man does? You are trying to sell me this good guy act, is this who you really are?" Jerica pauses from her heartfelt plea. "Is this your idea of a good man?" He doesn't hesitate to repeat what he has been saying to her. He whispers the mantra in an even tone. "I saw a need and I want you to genuinely consider my offer. This is not to hurt you. You fail to see things my way because you haven't been willing to open your mind to what my offer truly is."

At this point silence is the only answer. The nurse comes in and approaches Jerica and Jonathan with caution. "Mrs. Slack, if you begin to see spots or have an allergic reaction to any of the medications please call Dr. Walsh. His number is here in the paperwork." It's clear she has this spill memorized. Once the discharge papers are ready and the proper medications are prescribed to help her calm down and sleep, Jerica and Jonathan listen carefully as the discharge nurse gives more detailed instructions leading to the in-house pharmacy. Walking through the hospital, Jerica is dressed back into the same black dress and flats she left Jonathan's house in over a week ago. Sweat mixed with wrinkles and messy hair walking beside a very large man with the freshest lumberjack haircut and tight jeans look possible. Jerica isn't too happy with the way their conversation left off. She still hasn't come up with anything to say.

Now that they are alone and heading through the long hospital tension is building between them. "Jerica, slow down and talk to me." Jonathan coaxed quietly. "This is wrong, why don't you see that." Stopping in her tracks with tears in her eyes fighting to keep her voice down, Jerica answers his call. His face is stained with a scared look, but Jerica doesn't care. She stomped right passed him with her eyes fixed on the floor. People are staring but neither one seems to care. Tears fall from Jerica's already soaked wet cheeks. She looked up once and couldn't see through her lashes or beyond the puddles built up in her eyes, so she just followed

Jonathan.

Jerica felt defeated and scared. The ride home is silent. Jerica's mind is at work trying to find a way to escape. Replaying all of the events from the time of the accident to the time of the dinner that last night. There are so many parts missing. Jerica starts to feel overly frustrated. In silence her anger is festering. Angry and furious as the ride comes to an end, Jerica enters the house and it all starts. Yelling and screaming. No real words just sound. Her vision is blurred, and her body is hot to the touch with rage seeping from her pores. Jerica is not one to shy away from words, but she is at a loss right now not being able to translate her screams to what she is feeling. Slamming doors from room to room yelling, screaming, and seeing no end to this behavior. Right now, Jerica has so much to be angry about she can't or won't organize her thoughts.

Stopping in the family room where she has been followed by Jonathan. There are two single sitting chairs separated by a fury shag carpet. In front of a bay window is a large chocolate couch filled with chocolate and cream pillows. The walls are a deep tan color that compliments the very plush carpeted floor. There is a ceiling to floor, built in bookshelf which is the only thing that interrupts the room's expensive look. Jerica doesn't spend much time on her breathtaking surroundings.

"Five months." She finds her words which has leveled out no doubt after taking a true took at the room. Bile rises again. She raises her voice an octave higher. "Five months, what kind of sick sick sick bastard are you? How many times have you done this, huh, tell me, what number am I to this little obsession you have? Have I been in a coma this whole time? Who are you, do you rape children and imprison their mothers?" Jerica and Jonathan are now toe to toe.

Beauty and the Beast. The beauty is outraged and angry. The beast is a tall slender, plainly dressed, tired face, gray haired man. Suddenly it hits her, and she remembers babbling while she stood bloody on his stoop the day of the accident. This feels like the same babbling moment that she had before. The difference is this time she really sees his sadness. She doesn't care because she is sad too. He speaks.

"I would never lay a hand on any child. Creating the perfect family situation is my purpose for living. I need you and these kids to function. I am obsessed with giving all three of you everything you could need and want. Having to worry less about love and companionship gives you time to make impossible situations into possible ones. That is why I am a college professor. Each of my students that are struggling in any subject I am tutoring. I have taken on a lot caring for you and the kids. I see the situation and these kids growing up without a family in some foster care system along with you going back to Texas without a family would be devastating to us all. I had a lot of time to think the whole time you were unconscious. I would never hurt, hit, or sexually abuse you nor the children. You were put to sleep not knowing you had an allergy to aspirin and codeine. The meds made you sleep for far longer than anticipated. I even called a doctor here to care for you in that time to make sure you were ok. By the way your body needed time to heal without any of us seeing you go through the pain you were in for your broken bones and banged up face.

CHAPTER 13 : FLOODS MY HEART

Jonathan paused for just a moment trying to give her room to speak. Jerica looking down not engaging in this conversation at all. "Here's the thing. We all need this family for different reasons. I only once gave you either one of those medications because you were violent. I didn't want the children to see that. And to give you more insight to what number you are, you are only my second wife I've been married for the last fifteen years. My wife died a few months ago. Is this enough information for you to just go with it." He softly coaxes her to look at him. Staring her in her eyes he is trying to calm her with his soft voice as he raises his hand slowly to rub her shoulder.

Standing still in front of one another, his hand rest on her shoulder and he continues to try to convince her. "I am not the enemy; I knew this would be tough to deal with and I truly don't know what I'm doing but I know it's the right thing to do considering I have resources at my disposal to make your dreams in or out of your reach happen for you." His golden eyes and his golden skin both are playing a huge role in mesmerizing Jerica as if this is going to all of a sudden be ok. Jonathan phone chimes and Jerica wakes up. Quickly snapping out of it, Jerica takes a step back disconnecting herself from him. Knocking Jonathan's hand off of her shoulder breaking their contact, which was obviously forced on her part, made Jonathan angry but he didn't show it much. Only his face gives away his true feelings. The tone of his voice changes to something dark and evil, but still very quiet, "I did you a favor". Jonathan closes the space between them once again. This time catching Jerica by the elbow before she steps back in fear out of his reach for the second time.

Jonathan reaches in his pocket and Jerica gives subtle resistance fighting to get away from his determined hold. Pushing a few buttons on his phone Jonathan pulls Jerica close to his body releasing her arm and clutching her full body under his arm. She fits just as firmly and expertly as if he was holding the precious baby girl he kidnapped. He holds the phone out with his other hand as if he were taking a selfie. She whips her hair swiftly and her eyes flick towards the side of his face in disgust. Jerica still fighting and even harder now yelling out "this is so not the time for a selfie you freak!" Jonathan holds her even harder to position her to care for his reasoning as the sound spills from his phone.

She is stomping on his steel toe cowboy boots with all of her mite even though it doesn't affect him. He is stuck in the position he is in as she continues to fight. He calls her name rolling his eyes heavily. "Jerica!" She slows her tantrum until she is no longer fighting but fixated on the phone, he is holding out of her reach no doubt because she may have half a mind to break it.

It's a news article seemingly chiming as loud as his phone will go, "Hurricane Barbara is still wreaking havoc. There are now at least one hundred deaths related to Hurricane Barbara, after it dumped several feet of rain in a matter of days, Crittenden County News confirms, Starting in Houston with the worst flooding ever! Hurricane Barbara has the highest death toll in history. Many of those deaths confirmed in thirteen Texas counties happened when people were caught in quickly rising floodwaters or lost control of their vehicles on water-logged roads, emergency management officials said..."

The news broadcaster of the TV nineteen Crittenden County News Now station informs all its listeners about the storm that keeps on giving. It takes a few moments to put together the severity of the situation, but Jerica gets it. She is now reaching for the phone and as she snatches it, she drops to the floor, Jonathan letting go of the phone without hesitation. He knew this would nearly break her or make her more determined to leave and find them, however, he decides to lay everything out on the table now that she is back in the home with him and the children.

Walking away from Jerica, Jonathan makes his way to the doorway. Leaning on the panel of the wooden frame he watches her waiting for his opportunity to engage. Letting the next video start, "Please pray for Texas". This video is shorter. Celebrities speaking calmly urge people to give as much as they can to help authorities when paying first responders. People looking for their family and friends get into the waters looking to find all who may be hurt. Her tears are coming down nonstop, but they go unaddressed as Jerica sit limp on the floor still holding the phone. The video ends playing soft music as images flash the small screen of survival, heartache and pain. Jonathan still leaning quietly against the wall clears his throat.

Giving as much information as he knows, Jonathan adds, "your neighborhood was obliterated. You have nothing left to go back to. I sent a close friend there to give supplies and help to locate your family, giving the situation I was prepared to help you in any way I could you went rogue before I could speak to you." Jonathan pauses a brief moment as he reflects on the disaster. "About anything, really. At any rate, there was no luck in locating your family. Jerica, this storm is still going on, otherwise I would have given you more concrete information. For now, all I have is news articles. Authorities and rescue teams are not allowing anyone in the area unless you happen to be driving a tank. My guy is as close as he can get to the situation."

He pauses waiting for a reaction from Jerica that doesn't come. She dropped the phone and has pressed her knees to her chest crying softly as she lays on the soft carpet in her lush surroundings.

"Jerica, I wiped your identity and here you are able to start over. The only thing is, is the life I've created comes with two children that was also misplaced by an accident you caused, me and my dad. Again, I am not your enemy. This is not a punishment; this is a way out. We will not ignore your family; they can fit into whatever plan we come up with provided we find them safe."

This is too much for her to take in. Mind racing, rocking back and forth, body shaking, Jerica can feel her mind losing control. Too late, it was just too late to speak. The darkness has taken over. She is now asleep.

Flashes of the accident replaying like a motion picture movie. Something she either did not realize before or the fact that her subconscious is just now starting to put the pieces of the puzzle together, but there is a woman standing in front of her car. Jerica can see her mouth moving but cannot make out what she is saying. The woman's appearance is uncared for, strained and sick as she stands still in the middle of the street. As the flash reveals, Jerica is slowing down the car as she approaches the figure in the street. The motion picture is Jerica watching from outside of her car. The wandering woman turns her back as if to start to walk. Jerica slowly speeds back up thinking she will miss the lady crossing if she times it just right. Jerica contemplates slamming on her brakes, but as she watches Jerica notices the lady is not stopping. From inside the moving car Jerica reaches out to her. Jerica is shouting "no" at the top of her lungs as if she can stop this stranger from doing what she thinks she is about to do. This woman, this sick woman is positioning herself to be ran over! Her mouth moves and as Jerica runs towards the lady, she didn't recognize what the lady was saying at first but rain in the eye of a storm, Jerica realizes the words she is whispering is, "death rather than bondage".

The sound that Jerica will never be able to get out of her mind haunts her dreams as well. The sound of the car behind Jerica's slams into the back of her. Scenes are changing in her dream as if this is a real movie. The motion picture is revealing the scene as Jerica is walking away from the car to get help. Another piece to the puzzle and also to Jerica's surprise, the woman is smashed underneath Jerica's car. Startled and afraid, Jerica runs past her motion picture self-looking to try to save the woman. As she takes her last breath, she says to Jerica, "it's your turn."

Jerica jumps awake. She just lays there in a state of shock. Remembering her flashes and her pain while seeing what transpired. As unlikely as it has always been, Jerica awakes but still remembers everything her subconscious revealed. As her grandma always told her, "dreams are often messaging we never seem to understand". And with that, Jerica trust everything that was revealed, "but who is that woman?" She says out loud. "I know I have to lose the battle to win the war, but how?" Jerica continues to speak her thoughts out loud.

"I'm not sure, Jerica. I guess it depends on who and what you are talking about." Jerica jumps all the way up and wraps herself more tightly into the top cover from her bed. She searches the room to find Jonathan in the armchair in the corner where Robert is usually waiting to scare the hell out of her when she wakes up out of one of her mini but many commas. Sitting in complete silence for a few moments looking in each other's direction, Jerica's mind is going nonstop. Coming up with something that resembles a plan she speaks to Jonathan.

"I am going to shower and then I would like to speak with you" Jerica is putting her unprepared plan into motion. Jonathan slowly rises from the chair not taking his eyes off of hers. "Should I send dad and the kids away?" Jonathan has his eyebrows raised awaiting the answer not sure if this is going to be another turn up session or not.

"Yes, unless there is somewhere, we can talk in complete, uninterrupted quietness, I would like it if we could speak in private." Jerica answers in complete focus, no doubt trying to be cute while she buys time to execute her plan. "You are not giving much away Jerica." Jonathan is worried. She doesn't respond because she doesn't want to look like she is wasting his time in case she changes her mind.

Jonathan heads toward the door to prepare for this much needed conversation. "Wait, where do you keep the clothes that I can choose from to wear?" He gives his answer but clearly, he's annoyed. "Jerica, in the closet and every drawer here, you can find clothes among other things that may help make your stay here bearable." He lifts himself from the wall he was currently holding up. "By chance did you keep any of the things that was in my car?" Jonathan says he would have to ask his father, then turns and heads out the door, leaving Jerica to it.

There was not much thought given to her belongings as Jerica knows she has other business to tend to. Taking her time to really go through every drawer, Jerica finds all sorts of things. In a single dresser there is everything from fragrances to vibrators, sexy lingerie to plain old everyday underwear. "What is your angle Mr. Slack." Speaking her thoughts out loud fully knowing she is alone this time. She shakes her head as if trying to get rid of distractions and get back on track. She moves on to find something to slip into after her shower. After being blessed by the hot water and soft suds of the french vanilla dove soap, Jerica is ready. Physically and mentally ready for this much needed talk.

CHAPTER 14 : EXPECTATIONS

Heading towards the living room Jerica admires the paintings on the walls as she anticipates seeing him. Confused by the feeling in the pit of her stomach, Jerica is secretly admiring herself for the fight in her so far. Speaking of fight there is a smile that creeps across her face as happy thoughts of how much her father fought after his diagnosis with cancer. Making it to the living room, he isn't there. There is another room she has not seen before, the door is ajar and without contemplating going in, her feet think for her and takes her where she needs to be. Again, without her mind actually agreeing on a solid plan to go in, her feet are forcing her through the door. She it pushes it open and her breath catches.

She finds him seated in a chair that is next to a massive fireplace. His hair has a perfectly mixed silver and gold glow. The print on his shirt is a match to the dancing flames. The fire is lit and that is the only light in the entire room. There is another armchair that is identical to his. Separated only by a small table which has a glass bottle of wine perched in an ice bowl that has the same shine as his hair. The wine looks very expensive. The short table is lined with two glasses. There is an incense lit which smells very sweet. Jerica's plan to wave the white flag and hammer out the details of the arrangement is underway. Although this is her time to shine, she is very nervous. The feeling that resonated in the pit of her stomach before, makes her feel like throwing up again now.

Jerica slowly sits down on the side of her make-believe husband not getting relaxed but sitting straight up in the chair looking directly at the light given by the fire. Her stance breathes "stay focused and controlled". Her expression is not giving anything away. Looking at him squarely in the eyes radiating seriousness, nothing is distracting her now.

It's clear to Jerica all of his attention is on her. She starts to speak. "Let's talk about what I see. I set out to take a much-needed trip that would afford me great opportunities. The idea of my trip was shattered by the accident. Looking for help and was kidnapped. The children in the other car were also kidnapped. Only Lord knows what happened to their mother. I've been drugged, bathed, clothed and held tied to a bed for five months. Are you following me so far?"

Jonathan gives a simple answer. "Yes"

"There are choices made for me. I've been forced into something I did not ask for. My only family have been involved in a catastrophic hurricane with a pretty name and I am not even able to get to them because of the foolery you are constantly trying to force me into." Jerica continues.

"You do not know me well but for starters, I do not leave my family high and dry. They will be looking for me and I will look for them. If you do not see the value in me caring for my mother and sister, then you will never convince me that you want this family life. Which means we will not make it past this room without hell being served on a platter for the rest of your existence."

Jonathan's body language changes as he shifts in his chair. This could mean he is disgusted or waiting patiently for his chance to tear into her.

"You only get one chance beyond this room to lie or slip up and I am out." Jerica's eyes are fixated on Jonathan's, not wavering one bit. Body language still reeking of controlled confidence and determination. "I will ask you questions, and I require real answers, truthful answers. I will also let you know what my demands are in order to be in this arrangement which you should find peaceful. This is the time I expect you to iron out any duties or requirements you have of me which will also be heavily considered on my part to help me consider if I am going to agree with your idea of life here. Are you prepared to have this type of conversation right here right now?"

Jonathan gives a simple answer. "Yes"

"Starting now!" Jerica states with quiet apprehension about the announcement.

"You know as well as I do that, I did not cause that accident. There was a woman in the road that looked like she was crossing the street but when I approached her, she didn't give me time to think. Her mouth was moving like she was singing a song or something. Next thing I knew she was throwing herself in front of my car to hit her. This is what caused the lady and her kids to hit into the back of me. Since you and your father cleaned up the mess you should have seen that lady under my car. I see her under there when I was going to get help." Jerica exclaims squeezing as much attitude through her words as she can. "The woman was smashed to hell under the car, who was she? I'm sure she is tied to this in some way."

Jonathan tells Jerica he was by her side the entire time and did not see the accident, or the children's mother or the mystery lady underneath the smashed car.

"That woman wasn't at my doorstep as banged up as you were needing and accepting my help. She was not a concern to me, you were Jerica." Jerica's eyes started to water at the fact that the lady could have been alive. She couldn't dwell on the thought, there were other things on her list.

"I'd be a fool not to ask, so, is there a way I can have my new identity and live freely? I mean, I can walk right out of this door and never come back. If you are not stopping me from leaving what will happen if I do?"

Jonathan raises an eyebrow, "Darling, my

resources cooked you up, from your DNA to your bank account. There will be no you, without us. If you don't have me, I will strip you. I will strip Jewell Slack from the database, and you will never be able to get Jerica Stevenson back again, she is already gone. You may have the resources of your own that causes you to regain some other identity or you may just live as a homeless person if you want but nevertheless you will have no identity without me and the kids."

"What happened to the children's mother, was she really dead?" Jerica moved on rather quickly. Feeling her control of the conversation slipping, she was also realizing she knew the answer. "Again, Jerica, I was by your side the entire time. My father went out there and got the kids. I've asked my father these same questions, but he will not speak so there is no way for me to know. Although it may have been an original question, my true desire is not to know about anyone but you."

Jerica narrows her eyes in anger. "You know that answer is a bunch of bull." She tells him exactly what is on her mind. Giving him a taste of what he can expect for the rest of his life should she agree to this situation.

"Jerica, I understand you do not trust me but right here right now you are asking me all that you want to ask, and I am being truthful. You have to listen and as you stated if you find anything, I have told you to be a lie, you will have to do what you feel I deserve. What is the next detail of our arrangement would you like to hammer out?"

Jerica feels the urge to go into insane lady mode, but she doesn't. Getting down to some of the important questions Jerica is back focused.

"I want to know what you expect this arrangement to be. What is my role as wife and mother?" Jonathan starts to rub his knees. His movements are so slow they would be unnoticeable if Jerica wasn't watching his every move. For several moments he is contemplating his answer. His facial expression has gone from confused to satisfied and now to fear all in the matter of the hour she's been standing before him.

"I expect you to get up every morning with a fresh and polite attitude. Before you do anything or see any of us, I want you to get yourself together by reigning in your attitude. Meeting us for breakfast is a must, every morning. Spending time with the kids will give them a feeling that they have a mother. They will feel more complete to have your nature giving nurture. Also, if you have a problem with me it should be addressed in private. Coming in here gives me a sense of privacy. If we are to have sex, I would only like to do that in here. There is a room off to the side. Sex is not required but I hope. The end result should be you grow to love me and get comfortable enough with our arrangement that you want to offer your body to me. Even if you never move into my bedroom, I am here for you, regardless of the need."

Shaking her head at the thought of sex with an abductor is painful and highly unlikely. As the thoughts cross her mind, she starts twitching and scratching her arm like she has an unfulfilled addiction. Jerica is relieved because the thought of being so close to him had not fully crossed her mind. She wouldn't be able to bare it. He is a monster, no matter how much he claims he isn't. "We will never get to that point."

Moving on, Jerica has something to say that would probably not go so well with Jonathan. Truthfully, she wants a reason for this arrangement to blow up in his face. She doesn't know how Jonathan will feel about this situation, but Michael is a key part of her plan.

It all hangs in the balance on what Michael decides.

Without further delay, she starts the last point on her mental note that she has to get straight. Although she has been saying whatever comes to her mind thus far, she is confident that she is covering all of the important marks.

"Michael has to know everything about the arrangement. He is a key part to what we have. He is just a little boy and will have major holes in his life. You say you want a smooth sailing life and want everyone to be comfortable, this is something that will break the deal if you do not agree. I will not live here pretending to be happy if Michael is not on board. He is old enough to understand, I know this because we had a conversation about things that he saw and did since I have been unconscious thanks to you. He is very observant and it's not in my nature to be deceitful."

At this point, Jonathan is having a moment of panic. Body language is the dead giveaway but despite his reserves he says nothing. Quietly he asks, "what will happen if I do not agree to your terms?" She now sees why his body has betrayed him. He is questioning the power she has over this situation and her ability to make decisions for herself. "I will kill myself. Death is better than living in fear." Jerica states with glassy eyes and a definite tone. "But to live in F.E.A.R one has to die taking the doubt and the word [no] with them." Jonathan draws his breath and stands to his feet in a hurry. His voice is still quiet when he agrees to Jerica's terms. She starts spitting her other demands that are all less heavy than the others.

"You will not go into my room for any reason.

I will not be having sex with you under any circumstances.

You are not my man, so I do not have to obey you.

Do not expect me to bend or break any of my own rules."

Remember I am watching your every move and will not hesitate to do what is necessary for myself. Jerica list her last few demands while staring Jonathan directly in his soul. To be fair she asks was there anything else he needed to tell her about who he is or what he planned or is planning to do. He is still very quiet at this point; he doesn't want to say anything out loud which causes him to just give her a slight head shake no. "Do you agree with all that has come of this conversation?" Again, Jonathan lends another sign language nodding his head yes.

With Jonathan's easy agreeance, Jerica feels a sudden rush of anger added to the anger she has been repeatedly swallowing during this whole conversation. She is a volcano about to erupt. The predicament she has found herself in is disgusting. She can't seem to shake the feeling of rebellion and pettiness as they both sit there staring into the fire that flickers in reflection of their words and gestures.

"I should let you know that I don't want this to work. I feel backed into a corner and I hate it, I hate you. I have nothing, no one believes me, and the only way out is walking to campus or back to Houston until I find someone that can verify who I am and hopefully rebuild my life. I want you to go to jail for what you've done. I'm mad at myself because I don't know how to fight this. The slightest little screw up I see in you I will be lifeless and we both will suffer behind the misery you imposed on me and the kids. I'm watching you from this second on!" Tension is radiating off of Jerica is flood amounts. "Everything starts as soon as we have the family discussion and I'm sorry for the inconvenience of this situation. I saw a problem and I did what I thought would handle it. I will continue to stand by that." Jonathan tried to put a bandage over Jerica's wombs, knowing it sounds like b.s. Given the situation he doesn't blame her for feeling like she does.

"I wouldn't believe me either if I were you." He continues to try. He is looking into her eyes while she seems to be looking past him.

CHAPTER 15 : GET OUT

"GET OUT, NOW!" she screams as she sinks to the floor holding herself. Unhappy, bothered and speechless, Jerica is sulking. The look on her face unmask her hopeless feelings. She feels powerless in this moment. "I need a moment and then we will have a gathering to address whatever this is with all the members of this disaster we will soon all call a family." Jerica says as she watches Jonathan retreat closing the door as quietly as his steps were. The tears start immediately falling from her eyes. This time, she doesn't even attempt to control her emotions.

Crying out begging and praying someone

responds, Jerica doesn't hold anything back. "God, please order my steps, I know you will not bring me to something you don't intend to see me through. I know you are all knowing, and you will carry me through, but I am not strong enough. Help me to protect these children. Show me what my purpose is. In the name of Jesus, Amen." continuing to sob uncontrollably, Jerica continues to sulk.

"Mom, if you are here, I'm sorry that I wasn't there when you needed me. Please forgive me. I'm scared of what I am turning into. I'm angry and I'm afraid. Mom I will always love you and remember your teachings. Please tell Jam that I am thinking of her. Let her know I love her, and I love you."

After a breath and a short moment of silence, she starts to feel the sting of horror and cries out once again. "Mom, Mom, Mom." Jerica calls out believing in her heart someone is listening. Opening her eyes, she spots the drink that has been getting warm on the table that separated her from her new husband. Jerica takes the glass and drinks it until it's gone, not even taking a breath. Pouring another cup, she drinks one after another.

All thoughts of marriage, kids, storms, and

identity thief are drowned by the smooth taste of the liquid relief.

Jerica wakes up and it's clear the next day has approached. She is hungry and lightheaded. She eyes the empty bottle and the turned over glasses on the floor sprawled out beside her. In her hand she is holding another bottle that is not quite empty but also doesn't have a lid on it. "Where did I get this one from?" She looks around the room and groans when her eyes meet the fresh sunlight coming through the barely covered window. Coaxing herself to put her body in motion she remembers her conversation with Jonathan, and she knows this conversation has to happen with Michael.

Once to her feet she hears the soft noises beyond the door. "Come on Jerica, you can do this. Trust God and trust yourself." Eyeing the doorknob, the strength she didn't know she had starts to take over.

"Good Morning, everyone." Jerica greets everyone as she stumbles through the kitchen area. Making it into her bedroom she finds clothes have been laid out for her along with everything she needs for a shower. Beside her bed on the night stand she also notices a locked journal with a pen attached. "I guess this would help wouldn't it." Speaking out loud she knows this is final. Jerica's head began to pound, and she retreats to the bathroom. Stepping once again into the healing hot waters of Jonathan's home with the only difference being this start a journey of uncertainty.

Stepping out of the shower, Jerica is feeling slightly better. She knows she has to eat so she rushes to get on some clothes. Raiding the closet and drawers she finds a t shirt and some sweatpants and puts the clothes that was chosen for her back in the closet. Thinking for herself is mandatory. She reassures herself that she is in control of her own life, even down to the clothes she wears. Sweet thoughts of finding a way out of this swirl in the back of her mind as she dresses. Looking in the full body mirror, she recites an empowering message her mother used to tell her whenever she felt sad about any given situation, "Your mind is so powerful that your body cannot perform without it. People may not know your full potential but it's not their job to, it's yours. Now, go and be great."

Jerica heads in search of Jonathan to inform him of her plans for the next couple of hours. "Hello, I need to talk to you, do you have a moment?" she asks as nicely as she can. "I'm sorry for bothering you in your office but I am very hungry as you can imagine. I can fix my own food, but I was coming to let you know once I am done eating, I would like to discuss your work hours and when the best time to talk to Michael would be. If it is ok with you, I would like to have the first part of the conversation without you and then once we have had a chance to talk, we can bring you in and you can cover anything you feel you need to."

Jonathan's face tells Jerica he is very skeptical about her speaking to Michael alone. That dumbfound doesn't stop Jerica from starring in his face waiting for an answer. "I know you need to try to find a way to trust me so yes, of course you can talk to Michael alone. I have nothing to hide. You can talk to him as soon as you are ready. I will be here, and you can come get me once you are ready for me to come in. His room is the second door on the left. He has a flexible school schedule so he will be available whenever you are ready. Is there anything else you wanted from me for right now, I mean until then? Jerica shakes her head no. He is back in his office closing the door. As she walks away the brief thought crosses her mind wondering why he seemed to stumble his words. One growl from her stomach everything but food is forgotten.

"Knock, Knock" Jerica calls as she slowly approaches the door into Michael's room. Pushing the door again she calls out once more, "Knock, Knock." As she pushes open the door her expectations to what she felt his room should be were not met. To her amazement his room is large in size and neatly organized.

The walls are painted in a powder blue. Michael has a queen size bed with a blue comforter. The comforter matches the shade of blue on the walls. Six pillows line the headboard of his bed three all white and three white small light blue stripes in a horizontal pattern. The headboard is brown with a curvy pattern. Michael has five posters on his wall, two basketball, two baseball and one football. None of the posters were of any particular player, only of the local fields and of the general crowds. The overall view of the photos captures the support of the team. The crowds are painted in the team colors. Just by looking at these photos, you can see the amount of excitement the entire crowd feels.

His tall dresser has five drawers and is a bright red color with Christmas stickers on each drawer. Alongside the dresser sits his entertainment center that holds Michael's tv which is a flat screen forty inch that is turned off. Michael's tv stand is lined with comic books and a few paperbacks that seem to be age appropriate at first glance. There are about ten to twelve games on the opposite side of the shelf, all for his Sega dream cast which is housed in the middle of the shelf. There is a small carpet in front of the tv stand. As funny as it looks, there are football patterns that look a lot like someone splattered chili on an all-white carpet. The thought made Jerica crack a genuine smile. Michael's curtains have different color soccer balls and footballs along the top and bottom of each.

She finds Michael laying across the bed when Jerica walked completely in room. He was wearing headphones while watching Ronald's Cafe classic episodes on his iPad. Jerica calls Michael's name. He slowly turns around and his face lights up. "Hey Michael! I just wanted to talk with you for a moment, is that okay?" Jerica asked while slowly walking towards Michael's bed. "Sure, Ms. Jerica." Michael agreed while he removed his headphones and stuffed his iPad underneath his pillow.

"Hey, I just wanted to go over some things about staying here. I know from the last time we talked that you don't know what happened to your mother, is that still the case?" Jerica starts out slow. "Yeah, no one has even mentioned my mom since the accident."

"Look Michael, this is all weird for both of us. But I need to ask you some very uncomfortable questions just say yes or no. I will also give you some information that you may not understand. Just bear with me and I will move quickly. Michael doesn't give much away with his body language or words. Jerica starts. "Have you been touched in an inappropriate way?"

"No" Michael rolls his eyes at the question.

"Have anything happened to you here that make you feel afraid or uncomfortable and would you tell me if it did?" Jerica in turn rolled her eyes at his Michael rolling his eyes.

"No, not yet. Are you going to be around more now? You are always sleep and I sometimes need you." Michael begins his questions.

"Yes, I am going to be around more. This is why we are talking. I have agreed to stay here only if you will. Has anything happened that made you uncomfortable?" She responds a tenderly as she can.

"Everything is uncomfortable and weird. But I am not hurt. I'm okay." He doesn't hesitate to continue.

"This is not our home, we just met but Mr. Jonathan wants us to live here and not live anywhere else. He thinks it's best if I am his wife and you and sapphire become his children. I am here only to help you but if you want to leave, I will help you do that also. Do you want to leave, or do you want to stay?"

"Jerica, I want to stay here until my mom comes and get me and my sister. We may have family, but I don't know them no more than you or Jonathan. I know you helped us the night my mom got hurt and that I needed you so much to wake up."

CHAPTER 16 :

SHE MAY NOT COME BACK

The fact that Michael is staring Jerica directly in her eyes as if he was at one point mad at her is ripping her apart. She understands his terror and how much he needed her. That doesn't change the fact that Jerica need to find a way out.

"Michael, there is a chance that your mom coming back will never happen. I need to know if you are ok with your mom possibly never coming to get you. Over your time here I will learn all about your life before the accident and I will teach you about mine." Jerica gives Michael next steps.

Michael is given away by his shaky voice. "No one knows where my mom is and that scares me, but this house, Mr. Jonathan and you don't scare me. Will you protect me?"

"I will protect you. We will be best friends." Jerica hugs Michael and let him know Jonathan will be in to talk to him soon. To her surprise the smug face of Robert is waiting outside the door and Jonathan is beside him. Both rise from their comfortable stances on the wall looking directly into Jerica's face.

Without a doubt, Jonathan was listening outside the door. His relief is evident, no doubt from thinking that Jerica would try to sabotage the boy wanting to stay. "Showtime," Jonathan whispers as he passes Jerica in the hallway. The same smug look of accomplishment his father has. Jonathan walks in Michael's room wasting no time.

"Michael, Jerica is afraid I have hurt you or your sister and she just wants to make sure you are ok with living here. You having an instant family is nothing to be ashamed of. Sometimes the fairytale of life is the situation you create for the benefit of others as well as yourself. I am here to give you want you need in life. So, what you were not born to me I am here for you and that fact will never stop me. I just want you to know that we both just want what's best for you."

"I know, I understand, and I am willing to stay and make a life here until my mom comes back." Michael rebuts. "May I go back to watching TV now?"

Hanging on to what is right Michael doesn't hesitate to show Jonathan that he is still hoping for him mom to come back, no matter that Jerica has vowed to be there for him.

"Sure thing, let me know if you need anything as always."

Leaving from Michael's room in search of Jerica, there is no way Jerica can push back now. His smug look is gone and replaced with relief that Jerica will now find a way to do what's right and allow this family to happen. Jonathan finds her in the kitchen drinking water and pacing the floor. Her breath catches as she starts to look for what Jonathan is about to bother her with now.

"Here to gloat?" She says as he stops in front of her. "And so, it starts. What's for dinner?" He says dismissing her flustered look and protective attitude.

The next few months ago by pretty quickly. The holidays are moving along. The connection between Jerica and Jonathan is still void but the family doesn't seem to notice or even care anymore.

Over time Jerica has tried little things to test the waters with Jonathan like going grocery shopping without asking and taking the kids to the park. The only person, who raised so much of an eyebrow, is Robert. His creeping and standing where he shouldn't do seem to bother Jerica anymore because she knows her power.

All of this has been leading up to something. Jonathan is a smart man, so she knows not to put much past him. Jerica has been thinking over her plan in her mind for the last month. The idea of getting a job just for the holidays is the tip of the iceberg. "Jonathan shouldn't complain", she tells herself out loud in the shower. "My excuse is plausible. I want to be able to get my own money and figure out what I will get the kids myself for Christmas. Is that so bad? Yeah, if I am their mother why isn't that something to be expected?"

"Hey Ms. Jerica, what are you doing?" Michael questions her while stepping up on a stool by the counter.

"Oooooh nothing", she sings, "just fixing myself a snack, would you like one?"

"Please." He gives a simple answer while biting his bottom lip to keep from smiling. Perching himself up on a stool looking into Jerica's eyes while Jerica is reaching around the kitchen to add to the task at hand.

"Michael, I need to ask you a question about the day of the accident." She asks his permission before her line of questions begin.

"Did you happen to see a woman standing in the middle of the street when your mom hit the back of my car?" Michael is looking concerned as if he has been thinking about this same thing.

"Yes, I saw the woman and I know she ran into your car and she looked like she was hurt too." He says innocently and with a much softer and convincing tone.

"Thank you, Michael. I needed to know it actually happened." Jerica is now on the road to something new.

Jerica want to probe for more information on the deceased wife of Jonathan but doesn't want to raise any unnecessary suspicion and disturb the quietness of the home while her plan to leave is still being drawn up and laid out. As these thoughts are arising Jonathan appears in the doorway of Jerica's room as she lays stretched out on her bed thinking.

"Hey, I was just coming in to let you know I will be stepping out for a moment to have a drink or two. Would you like to come along for some fresh air?" Jonathan looks his regular ole regular self while asking as humbly as he can. "Nah, not this time. I will have to take a rain check. Have fun."

Jerica had to decline his offer no matter the real fact being that she really wanted to go. A little adult fun would be great at this point in her life. This gave her time to snoop around and try to gather information for her end game, pointedly, a name or a picture of the wife that made him a widower. In his absence would be the perfect time. We all need to know the real answer behind his obsession. He was married for fifteen years then this could be grief and if it is, he is not going about it the correct way. Jerica is determined to get down to the bottom of whatever is happening.

CHAPTER 17 : SEARCH WARRANT

The search turned up nothing. "This is a sign." Jerica spoke out loud. She went from place to place in each room of the house and came up with nothing. For a moment, she thought she was not giving herself enough time overly worried that someone would come in and find her snooping. Although, as usual, no one in the house was bothered with what she was doing. "By now I'm sure everyone thinks I'm crazy anyway." She says before she can keep the words from escaping her lips to add to their labels and judgements.

There was not a trace of the woman that has been spoken of in such a painful way. It's like she was scrubbed out of view. "Could what happened to me have happened to her?" The thought brings up a very good point that Jerica couldn't help but entertain. As she is looking around Jonathan's study undressing every inch of the room with her eyes, "who wants a reminder of the pain they endured or the void they feel?" Heading towards the door still using her words. "Watching her wither away and die, Jerica, get real, you've dealt with more taking on the role of your father when your father's life ended. On to the next thing. Abort mission." Jerica is wearing a housecoat which looks more like a silk cardigan with a green maxi dress and her hips sway with huge attitude as she exits Jonathan's living space.

Each room Jerica stopped in gave a new perspective on her mission and what it would really mean if she succeeded in her move. She thought about never again being able to take the easy road out. Never being able to come back to this life. All she needs is one person who recognizes her.

While Jerica is encouraging thoughts on the level of leaving, she also puts everything else into perspective. Counting out what's important she is rummaging through drawers in his office and takes the conversation from her head to her lips, "Michael is still looking for his mother to come back and get him. I'm still paying for a mistake that wasn't my own. These children have family and we need to find them. For the first five months I was drugged and kept tied up when my mother and sister were possibly somewhere dying. Yes, I need to find out about my family."

After a few hours of going all the way back over the house and still turning up nothing, Jerica turns into the next phase of her night and return to her room. Thinking out loud and writing in her journal, Jerica thinks she has a plan to escape.

The first step in her plan is to let Michael know she will be leaving in search of her mother and sister and as soon as she can get someone to believe her story about the accident and the kidnap, she will be back for him. There are unshed tears in his eyes when she tells him what she has planned. Nevertheless, Michael agrees to keep their secret to himself.

Leaving him is harder than she expected. The way she will be leaving is the questions now. Putting the last thoughts on this plan out loud to herself she admits, "sounds crazy but I need to commit a crime." Jerica has a plan to have Jonathan strip her of her identity which will spark Arkansas's judicial system to try harder to reach out and find some evidence of her existence prior to the accident and new identity. "This will work. Trust the process. Believe." she states to try and empower herself.

It didn't take her long to come up with the way she would leave with no trace of her given identity. First, came the argument. Jonathan asked Jerica to go out for drinks once again with him and his friends. Jerica chose this time in particular because for the life of her she can't understand why he invites her out into public to give them both the illusion of being in a real marriage. She tells him she wants to leave again, and he can strip her of her identity. She tells him she doesn't care, and she will not fight for the kids until she is stable. No surprise he starts to question her. "I am not willing to live this lie anymore. I want someone whom I can love without limits and have a real family. My own family. I want to be able to be put at ease as only my real husband and do. Just let me go."

She has cut him to the core with her choice of words. "I want to be your real husband. I want to be able to touch you. Everywhere. I respect your space and don't press my luck. I can do and be what you want me to be. Wouldn't it be easier for you to just let me?" He has adopted this painful look in his eyes, and it adds an uncomfortable heavy atmosphere to the hallway where they both stand slouching.

"There is nothing I want from you. Did you forget that I am your slave? Did you forget you've created this fairytale of a life? Did you forget your real wife died? I will always be a situational fetish for you. We will never love each other. You will always have a forced relationship." Jerica isn't holding back. No parts of this tolerance she's built for him has allowed her to actually feel anything genuine.

He steps aside without further argument and she leaves.

Remembering the pity money, she has in her pocket; Jerica is able to launch her plan. She goes into a local bar and drinks enough drinks to sour her breath and her mood with a very bad attitude. Slurred words and wavering feet give reason for the bartender to put Jerica in a cab. Once the cab arrives, she does not want a man to touch her and causes a scene.

"Ma'am, what is going on here?" A rawled voice comes up from behind Jerica startling her no doubt instantly thinking Jerica was the one who needed help. "Look you bastard, it's an officer of the law." Jerica twirls her finger around in the officer's face as she falls into his arms. "Never mind, I see what the problem is. Let's go, we are going to for a ride."

After the fact, Jerica commits an actual crime of urinating in public. "Hopefully this doesn't get me real jail time." she says out loud, but the officer doesn't say anything to her. All of this in order to get a twenty-four hour hold for public intoxication. "Well, at the very least it worked." She tries her luck one more time, but she still doesn't get a response. "I have no choice but to sing since you won't talk to me!" she states using her liquid courage as an excuse to let loose. Jerica starts to bellow Fire and Desire on any other occasion sung by Rick James and Tina Marie.

The police arrive at the station and since she never leaves the house, they truly have no idea who she is. The ride was noticeably less than comfortable and there was more tugging and pushing than necessary during the arrest, but first part is complete but at this point, the deed is done, and it is time that we start to clean up this mess.

"When will I be able to talk to a judge?"

Jerica drummed up in her mind, the bright idea to ask as she is disclosing her name and other asked questions to help them book her on the arresting charges. "Ma'am, please provide me with your name and I will tell you after you are booked what our procedures are." The officer is now raising her voice. "My name is Jerica Stevenson. I am from Darling, Texas. No, I do not have a driver's license or any identification with my name or picture on it." Jerica slurs out from her drunken state. "When can I see the judge, pay my fine and get out of here?" There is a hint of fight in her voice as she demands answers despite being ignored. Her point was to make them see and hear her which means she will not calm down.

Jerica stomps her foot and squared her shoulders. "Ma'am, you will get to see the judge Tuesday, seeing how today is Thursday you have a few days to think about your actions before you can get a fine and or a public defender." Officer Adams suddenly has this sympathetic look on her face as she speaks no doubt in response to Jerica's rapid relax in her shoulders which is accompanied by a look of sadness. Jerica is where she wants to be but did not anticipate the way she would feel being surrounded by concrete.

After the strip search, shower, picture, fingerprints, signing a trillion documents while enduring fast talking and a spitting Officer Adams, and then being led to a dark corner down the hall from the booking central retrieving the blankets and mat from a stack on the cold hard floor, reality set in for Jerica.

First, she is taken to a holding cell where she awaits a cell. The front of the room along both sides of the door is all plexiglass. The see-through walls give her a feeling of anxiety from the illusion she can just walk right through there and get out. Off in her daydream of leaving, Jerica is startled by a male officer that hits the glass yelling for Jerica to come and make her phone call. Jerica gets up from the metal bed and waits for the door to buzz for her to open.

"It's been a while since I've seen one of these", she mentions as she picks up the black receiver. Jerica calls the house number her mom has had since she was a little girl not hoping to talk to anyone. She briefly remembers Jonathan telling her he sent someone to look for both his mother and sister. The search was unsuccessful and the phone rung repeatedly.

"Thanks for thinking of us but we are not home so just leave us a message and when house phones become popular again, we may listen to it and call you back." Jerica hears her own voice loud on the voicemail with her mother screaming at her in the background telling her to behave. The sound of her mother's voice gut punches her almost to the floor. She slams down the phone receiver and walks back towards her holding cell. Picking up the long pant legs of her jumpsuit, Jerica ignores the fact that the door opened so easy.

CHAPTER 18 : DAY 1 OF JAIL

Jerica stares around the cell as eleven other women stare back at her. Quickly accessing there are only ten beds. There is an instant regret. "Jerica, you knew the first day was going to be hard." Jerica whispers to herself as she stomachs feeling out of place. These women and one man are dishing looks around the room at each other and then back at her. One annoying voice shout, "you aren't alone so don't look as if you don't know how this happened'. She rolled her eyes inwardly in disgust and continued to stare back at the big mouth.

Taking a moment for a few deep breaths, she looks at each corner of the concrete room she has found herself in. No cushion to speak of. Jerica is not feeling too good. Sick to her stomach, actually. Finally walking away from the spot she's been standing in since being shoved into hell, she finds a place to sit around the steel table in the middle of the room. With everyone staring at her, she stops admiring the room and tries to find something to stare at.

The guy sitting to her right decides to spark up a conversation. His wavy man bun indicates he may not belong here. "Hangover out of this world, huh?" Him just mentioning the words causes her to feel it even harder. Jerica doesn't answer; she just rolls her eyes involuntarily. Finding a home for her eyes, they rest on the television playing overhead. It doesn't take her long to notice the time in the bottom right hand corner. It's close to 4:30 pm. She has been in jail since 7pm last night. Snatched out of her internalized pity party, everyone draws their attention to the loud clicking sounds of the lock on the heavy door. "Jerica Stevenson, please approach the door and put both hands and wrists inside the opening in the center of the open window. Make fist and insert palms up." Everyone is looking at her once the loud demanding voice starts to speak its rehearsed lines. Jerica, with protesting body parts, approached the door following the directions.

Once out in the hallway, she is escorted to the holding area which she barely recognizes from her initial intake process. "Ms. Stevenson, I need you to verify that we recorded all of your information correctly. We are having trouble locating any information on a Jerica Stevenson."

Officer Adams is back on the case of the drunk and disorderly. Jerica spits out her name, date of birth, social security number, and last known address. "Well looks like all is correct. Have you ever gone by any other names?" Officer Adams looks lost while she shakes her head at her computer monitor. Feeling very afraid of what is happening, Jerica shakes her head no. "My identity was stolen at one point a few years ago; can you check records for my mother JoAnn Stevenson and my sister Jameria Stevenson?" Jerica recites their permanent address in Houston and waits for a response but all she gets from Officer Adams is, "take her back. Jerica, you will know something when I know something."

Back in paradise everyone seemed to have settled down. That was all of the excitement Jerica was rendered for the rest of the night.

The loud mouth points Jerica in the direction to her bunk. As unattractive as these walls are staring at them makes rethinking every mistake, she made in the years she's been living easy. Matters of the heart and soul has Jerica going between anger and sadness in her mind and there is no end to this discomfort.

CHAPTER 19 : DAY 2 OF JAIL

Seems like this plan isn't working at all. It may even be backfiring considering Jerica's state of mind is being challenged. The police have asked all sorts of questions to figure out her identity. This last round of questions gave Jerica hope because Officer Adams found information on both her mother and her sister. Jerica is still nowhere to be found in any database. Nothing has worked to find Jerica's identity. Frustration is settling in for her. With the worst anxiety building up, Jerica reminds herself that this is only day two. Repeating the mantra that she has continuously whispered to herself to keep encouraged, Jerica says it once again, "Even though you are here and doing nothing doesn't mean Officer Adams is out there doing nothing. Keep calm and stay focused on the goal Jerica." The best idea Jerica has had is to fall asleep and they will come and get her when they have something. That or either they can come get her to ask more probing questions, which will give her something to do. "Movement is good." She professes out loud causing some of the ladies she lives with to look in her direction. The predictions are eating away at her. Jerica is now realizing she need to lay down and try to sleep some of this anxiety away.

The sound of the heavy door lock sounds throughout the entire cell. The crack in the barred window creates sound and it causes Jerica to jump from her coma. "Jane Doe, Jerica Stevenson?" Eyes are visual through the dark window looking from one corner of the room to the next undoubtedly trying to spot Jerica out. "Up and on your feet. Approach the door." The voice is louder this time. "On my way." Jerica says in an unexercised cranky voice before the guard starts all the hollering over again.

"Where am I going?" Jerica asked as she is being shoved against the wall and handcuffed. "Quiet, inmate!" The guard says as if his day is ruined by having to do his job. He is alone which is rare, and he isn't wearing that annoyingly dusty blue hat like the rest of the guards she's seen. Jerica decides not to say anything else. She is escorted to a room with a huge glass mirror and a steel table. The table needs to be cleaned but Jerica is forced to touch it as her handcuffed wrist are now anchored to a hook connected to the table. Jerica is starting to feel anxious all over again. The guard walks around the table and sits across from Jerica. He is around Jerica's height and looks mixed with black and white. His uniform doesn't really fit him all that well and he looks angry. "What is your name, ma'am?" He dives in with questions. "Jerica Stevenson, sir. And it's not going to change." Jerica squared her shoulders and straightened her back.

I am not trying to change who you are or who you think you are. I want you to know that Officer Adams have been finding a lot out about how you got here and why you are trying so hard to leave. I am here to let you know if you are Jerica Stevenson, your name may be in connection with an accident. Do you know I'm referring to?" Jerica gives a slight nod without saying anything. "Words will be thrown around such as murder, disappearance, hit and run accident. I feel it was only fair that I advise you of these things. I would hate for someone in your position, broke and not much family, to be caught up in a no-win situation."

The guard is not giving much emotion away. Jerica makes a move to stand but is limited because of the restraints. "Take me back to my cell." Jerica is screaming to the top of her lungs. The guard says nothing but does exactly what she asked for by taking her back to her cell. Everyone is still up and staring at her as her plunges into her bed.

CHAPTER 20 : DAY 3 OF JAIL

Waking up to chatter at 4 am will never be received in a nice welcoming way. Jerica turns over with bad breath and an angry look on her face. Trying to keep it cool Jerica turned her back towards the group of girls not caring what they are actually doing. She doesn't want to look at anyone. Today is Sunday and most of all the girls have sentences they are carrying out, so they are allowed to work. Working means they can leave on Sundays and gather in the courtroom. Perks of being in trouble.

When she woke up mid-morning, she asked one of the girls where everyone was going. The guard yells at Jerica to leave the other inmates alone and go back to sleep. Only after he was gone did she find out the girl would be going to get the courtroom nice and clean for court early on Monday morning. "You reap what you sow, don't you? Cleaning the courtroom for the same judge that will keep you locked up like an animal in an overcrowded jail cell." Jerica is grumbling as she brushes her teeth.

Monday court is for drug dealers, probation/parole hearings, and other repeat offenders. Sunday the female inmates get to knock the weekend dust off of the oak tables and the nice leather chairs around the courtroom. "I will be glad when you'll shut up." Jerica calls out in a bad mood. She can hear some of the chatter as the ladies is coming back. "She never says much but when she does, she's a complete..." She overhears some of the girls in the room talking and she turns her head towards their voices.

"I heard she is lying about who she is", one of the girls standing in the group has no shame in her speculation and even less shame in her eagerness to gossip.

"Well if she thinks that will stop them from throwing the book at her pretty face, she is sadly mistaken." Her accomplice matches her cattiness. "Maybe we should tell her to cut that act before there are more charges brought against her and she becomes one of us." The girl adds as if it's her problem to fix.

When the females notice Jerica paying attention to their conversation one of them gets upset. The smaller one jumps up getting in Jerica's face. "If we were talking to you, you would know it. You are in jail not on the playground. If I catch you in my business again that pretty little face will have a reason to cover up."

Jerica is barely affected by the aggression shown by this woman who is nearly a foot and about 12 pounds less than Jerica. "Yeah ok, if I hear you talking about anything concerning me, which is not your business and you aren't talking to me, we will have to see whose face will need a cover up then." Jerica is still pissed from this morning.

Smallfry gives a smirk and steps back. Throwing up her hands and lowering her voice a little "look, a few people were questioning why you were still here after being taken out of here a few times and only in for pissing yourself on the sidewalk. I'm telling you, the longer you play this name game is the longer you stay here. I am only telling you this to help you."

Jerica is not feeling this conversation right now so all she can do is walk away. She feels like she said what she needed to say. Smallfry however, felt disrespected and ignored and felt like getting her point across. Smallfry grabs Jerica by her hair and down to the ground they go.

"To be honest all I heard was a lot of yelling and you guys rushed in. I did nothing to that girl." Jerica yells as she is being taken away.

Jerica is now in a wet concrete room alone. Her clothes had been taken away and she has not had a bath since she has been there. Just thinking about the conditions and what she sees overall has taken her off her focus. "I was not the aggressor!!! I was not the aggressor!!!!" She chants over and over again screaming at the top of her lungs. She gets no response, only the echo of her own voice. What seems like hours goes by not a word. Now, Jerica is hungry and grows more afraid by the minute. Thinking to herself what can she do, she begins to tell a story.

"Once there was a woman graduated high school, lost her father, and took on the responsibility of breadwinner in her family. This girl takes care of her sister and mother without complaints. Once she saved enough money for her family to survive a few years with little struggle and her sister graduated high school then shortly after started college, this woman decided to enroll in college herself. On the day of her trip to the college grounds to find a job and an apartment, she was involved in an accident never to be seen again." Cries and loud screams fill her cold empty cell as Jerica releases her truth.

"Who am I? I know who I am but my identity has been stripped. My identity is untraceable. I am now untraceable. I may not ever be able to prove who I really am but I want you to know I am not this person. I don't want to fight and be angry. I am kind, giving, God fearing and humble. Can anyone hear me? I give up. Did you hear me, I give up. Jonathan you win. I will play along. I accept being kidnapped and trapped with an untraceable identity." Her cries turn in to anger then to tears of sadness.

Jerica must have cried herself to sleep because she wakes startled by the sound of the lock of the heavy door. Food is shoved from what seems to be under the door. The door never opened but then again how would Jerica even know, it's so dark her eyes couldn't adjust to see what was going on. Everything happened so fast.

Jerica can now say she knows what it feels to have regrets. She could have asked about the time or what day it is. She can't see the food but she eats it as her mind races with her should've could've would've. She has never been so hungry in her life. Thinking out loud because she knows no one can hear her or if they can, they will never respond. "I have chosen this moment in time over what could have been. How could I have been so stupid to believe I could fight my way out of the horror I've been subjected to. Anything is better than this."

Sitting in her provided sports bra and boy short panties on the cold wet floor Jerica can't help to think anything could be better than this. At least at Jonathan's she had a warm bed, food she could eat whenever she got ready, children she could see and hug and smile at whenever she got ready to, and light to cherish although at this time she realized how much she took it for granted. She knows what she has to do now.

It's settled.

CHAPTER 21 : MAD AT THE WORLD

As what appear to be police officers are dragging her down the never-ending hallway with lights. She has clothes on, but how. Mumbling, Jerica ask "What is going on? Where are you taking me? Who told you to touch me?" Demanding answers but no one is responds. Passing her reflection on the windows, Jerica see how dirty she is.

Another window in passing reflects the bruising on her face and shoulders. Jerica is shook to her core by her reflection.

Emotionally drained she is at the end of her rope. The idea passes through Jerica's mind that with the pull Jonathan has in the community she is confident every charge will go away. Jerica knows she will have an attorney that will clear her all up and even get pain and suffering although Jerica is the one to blame for the injuries sustained. These thoughts make her sick to her stomach. She is not in a good place mentally and she knows it. There is nothing she can do about her situation right now. Her feelings are genuinely crushed. There is no more hope in her eyes or heart. She has been defeated.

Sitting Jerica down in the familiar chair she has been sitting in while being grilled repeatedly about her identity. Before being asked for any of her information again, she says, "My name is Jewel Slack, call my husband Jonathan Slack he will verify my identity and clear this whole thing up."

No other details mattered to Jerica at this time. She doesn't care what the day or time is. She doesn't care what happened to the other girl because she was the clear aggressor. Nothing matters except her leaving there. The visibly broken woman cannot pay attention to what is being said, everything sounds like people stepping on hundreds of empty eggshells. Those sounds are even fading away as the seconds pass.

Jonathan gets to the courthouse and asked to

speak to Jewels in private. "Why are you playing games with me? What have I done to you so horrible that you hurt my feelings and you storm out on the kid's and my life?"

"Jonathan you win, you told me what would happen and here I am in jail feeling hopeless and no one believes me." Jerica tries to articulate how she feels.

Jonathan is cold and heartless with a hint of exhaustion in his answer. "I can't trust you. And I know you do not trust me so why should I put up with the back and forth?"

"You don't have to; leave me here if it suits you." Jerica shouts. Jonathan is taken aback, and his facial expression gives away his stunned reaction. "What do you mean leave you here? I chose you and I want you, but I will not force you to live comfortably." Jonathan's words are cool but direct. He is not here to beat around the bush at this point. Jonathan wants her and is not afraid to say it. "Jerica, I need you. Do you understand that?"

And there it is, exactly what Jerica was looking for, her way in. "Well, isn't it enough that I had them find you and call you to rescue me?"

"Yes, that is plenty." Jonathan sounds convicted when he answers. He is looking down at the hands like a scolded child.

"Stop talking and take me back to the place you call home, now."

The silence in the car could measure with the sound of a butterfly needle dropping on faux fur carpet. There is nothing to focus on but the scenery which relaxes her. Lights, cars, airplanes, birds, trees, buildings and the sound of high winds all keeps Jerica from saying anything.

Not really seeing this coming but anxiety builds up in Jerica's stomach and she yells, "let me out. Stop the car. I want to walk the rest of the way." Jonathan slows down the car and without saying so further, Jerica jumps out and starts to breathe slower. This is due to the tight confinement of the punishment palace of Crittenden County. A Jerica set out not really knowing where she is going but Jonathan doesn't leave. He is traveling slowly behind her. He stops occasionally giving her the chance to figure out where she is going next.

She is not well. Very weak from being drunk then beat up and locked in a wet hole naked, she decides she's had enough. Waving at Jonathan he pulls up beside her and hops out to open her door for her. No matter the other cars that are honking at him for slowing them down. Once she is in, he lets down all of the windows in the car to help her stay calm. It works until they get back to Jonathan's home. Her home.

She arrives at the house. Stepping out of the car in the garage she notices the smell of freedom. Thoughts of the children and their health crosses her mind in a rushed panic but Jerica can only focus fully on getting the stink of the cold, wet jail off of her.

It takes a couple of days before she can stand on her own two feet. Robert, Jonathan and the kids have been so helpful to her.

After Jerica takes a bath and gets herself outwardly back to normal, she decides to write in her journal to free her mind of her failure to find her and Michael's family. After about an hour, her door creaks open. "Ms. Jerica, may I come in?" Michael is at the door, smiling as he sets eyes on Jerica. She nods and waves for him to come on in. Michael jumped on the bed where Jerica sat and gave her the biggest hug yet. "I'm glad you are back. I've missed you. I often wondered if you were ok. I asked Jonathan if I could call you but he said you didn't have a phone. I'm glad you are back. Are you okay?"

Michael spit out question after question. His adoration is obvious. "Yes Michael, I'm just fine. I am glad to be back here with you as well. I have some terrible news to share though. The plan didn't work. I was unable to find anything out about my family or yours. I have no news and we both may be stuck here for the long haul."

Jerica released Michael to gauge his reaction. The little boys face is questionable. "Ms. Jerica, I am just glad you are here back with us. I couldn't imagine losing another mother."

That admission stunned Jerica. Not wanting to sour the moment she said nothing. In her mind is where she did all of the talking, "I am not your mother, your mother was viciously taken from you by some deranged woman and possibly covered up by the men that live here who have sworn to take care of you." Jerica serves Michael up a smile and he tells her Robert told him not to bother her for a long time because she needed to continue to rest for a few more days. He leaves promising to be back before his bedtime.

Jerica is instantly mad. Writing it all down like a list, she tells her journal all about it after

Michael is out of the room.

I'm mad...

Mad because Michael needs a mother figure.

Mad because my idea for my life is now shattered by the obsession of a person that randomly chose someone's life to screw up because of his own heartache.

Mad because of the selfishness of the same human being.

Mad at the corner I am backed into.

Mad at the setup of my new life.

Mad that there are holes in this story.

Mad that no one knows me.

Mad for missing opportunities to ask questions and be more persistent.

Mad that I am afraid to try again.

Mad that I lost hope.

Mad because the darkness in jail broke my spirit to fight.

Mad because jail did nothing for my situation but make it worse.

Mad that I was born.

A few more days have passed, and every moment of those days have been filled with hatred and regret from Jerica towards Jonathan and his dumb father. All Jerica can think about is how much she has sacrificed for people in her life and how little she has ever received in return. She turns to writing again adding to the list.

Mad because my dreams lied to me.

Mad because there is truly no way out.

Mad because I am the one who always loses.

Mad because there is not a mean bone in my body.

Mad because I am not a fighter.

Mad because I make everyone else's life easier but my life is shit.

Mad at the kids.

Mad at the old man.

Mad at Jonathan.

Mad at this house.

Mad at the car.

Mad at the shower head for being so perfectly warm.

I'm mad that I don't have the balls to kill everyone in this house just to get back to who I am!!!!!!!!

CHAPTER 22 : I HATE YOU

Another week has gone by and Jerica is still angry at the world. At this point she knows she is mentally unstable but it's hard for her to care. Her focus is on the one thing she understands. Anger.

Jonathan kneels beside Jerica's bed accessing her mood before he speaks. The days are getting longer, and she is growing more distant from the family. Everyone is worried. His point of going into her room is to tell her as much. For moments he kneels without saying anything.

"Jerica, what can I do to help you? What is the problem? You are killing me with this anger." He starts out but pauses to gauge her reaction so far. "You wake up hateful, you go to bed hateful." He tries brutal honesty first because that is the kind of woman she has been up until this point in her life. "Please tell me what can I do or what should I do to help you transition back into this life? We were doing so well before you started to second guess our life. I want to help." Jonathan is almost in tears pleading with Jerica and his voice raises with every question he spits towards her.

Standing there in her anger she begins to speak in the lowest, coldest tone she can muster. "I hate you. You are a fake son of a bitch. Everything you have said to me isn't true. You told me you wanted me happy, but you force me into a fairytale life that doesn't fit who I am. You have taken me away from me and expect me to be Jewel. I hate you."

Jerica's voice is rising as she continues to tell him her true feelings. "I am miserable. I am suffering. I want my family. I want to start and finish school. You took that away from me. You hold all of my cards and I hate you." Jerica charges full force towards Jonathan. Catching her body against his, he doesn't try to stop the blows. He allows her to punch his face and chest. Striking him directly in the ear, her ring draws blood from his lobe. Jonathan is unaffected. He continues to let her release her anger.

Out of breath Jerica is screaming how much she hates Jonathan while he leaks blood from his face nose and ear. "I hate you; I hate you; I hate you; I hate you." Still standing in the same spot taking each lick as it comes, he is falling to the ground as she unleashes her pain onto him.

Jerica hears faint words, "what can I do, what can I do," she stops. His cries are sincere, and she is not this person. No more kicks or punches from her. Jerica takes pity and steps back from Jonathan. Louder she hears him say as he sobs. Tears and blood at the same time drop from his chin to his neck, chest and through shirt. It's so much blood. So many cuts." Jerica spoke out loud right before she threw her hand over her mouth.

He looks up at her and asks the question, "Are you ok?" To stop the blood from getting in his eyes he looked down yet again waiting for her response. Jerica looks him in the side view of his face, kneeling slowly down beside him and says without remorse. "I still hate you."

Jonathan lifted his face to meet her gaze. She stands back up in her defensive stance. Jerica drops her hand back down to her side. "I see your face and I get angry all over again. I see you first with compassion but then anger because I am your prisoner."

Jonathan moans out "what can I do. I need you with me. It's not an option anymore; I've paid a high price." He winces from the stab of pain from his words.

Walking to the bathroom to get a towel because he is dripping all over her floor, she has time to think. She hands over the towel and stares at him without saying a word. He sits down on the ground steadying himself so he can start the cleanup of his cuts. There is a hole in the bottom of the door where Jonathan was pushed into while trying to hold himself steady when Jerica wouldn't let up on the blows.

Not looking her in the face he asks again, "What can I do?" He doesn't care about consequences and he tells her as much. "Whatever it cost I will do it. However long it takes, I will work towards that single goal until my last breath. Please, tell me."

"Kill him", she demands. "Since my life has to be sacrificed for your happiness, you have to sacrifice a life also" she continues.

"Because you took it upon yourself to take my identity, Mr. Jonathan, now it's your turn to sacrifice a life. Oh, but there is more. You ask what you can do, you can suffer with me. If you want this life to be happy, you stoop to the same gutter you have me living in." Jerica continues.

"You have a choice, kill your father which will give you the equality you want in this relationship. I will even give you sex. You can have me. No more fighting. I will be here to serve you as you see fit."

"What is the other choice?" Jonathan has made no effort to wipe any of the blood or tears from his face since Jerica has made her announcement. Jerica doesn't care. She has a hole where her heart should be.

"The other choice is, you don't kill your father and remain superior to me by way of your happiness and I kill both children and then myself. Plain and simple but it's your choice."

Jonathan raises his voice once again. "Your unhappiness makes me unhappy. Can't you see that?"

"I don't care what you feel, you asked me, and I answered. Now what?" Jerica says watching Jonathan get up from the floor to stand over her.

Jerica's threats seem believable both to herself and to Jonathan by the look on his face. She is truly at the end of her rope with this whole situation. Life is not worth living if she is miserable and they both have some decisions to make about this failed arrangement. Every attempt at sanity she has tried hasn't worked and now she has to move on knowing she will never get out. The "her" that she was, is no more. She has an untraceable identity.

Four days of continued anger now from Jonathan and Jerica. Both are standoffish with the family. Jerica moving quietly from room to room watching every move the children make. Making sure there is no evidence of retaliation for her request.

Robert seems like he doesn't know what is happening. The kids are clueless as well. No clothes have been missing from the drawers and no one making a run for it. Not that Jerica can see anyway.

Jerica walks into Jonathan's office

unannounced as if she owns the place. As he drags his eyes away from the computer screen, she notices he has tears streaming down his face. Bending down to put her mouth close to his bandaged ear, she whispers to him, "aww, don't cry, you created this monster."

Jerica runs her hand down his shirt, down passed the belt buckle on his pants and crushes his cock in her hand and whispers, "your choice but you are running out of time. Two days or the fun begins."

"What happened to you in jail? You are getting more heartless by the minute." Jonathan chooses his words wisely. "Two peas in a pod then, you and me. Forever and no take backs." She rebuts still putting her voice low and daring in his head. Treading carefully, he tells her to get out. Looking her squarely in the face, tears are no longer streaming, "get out, now." He means it and Jerica decides to listen. As she walks toward the door, she leaves him with her last declaration of the truth in this situation, "I can see you are already getting to a point where you feel as angry as I do."

CHAPTER 23 : HIM OR US

The moment she leaves, Jerica realizes she has gone completely rogue. The situation will put them even. She focuses on that. She tells herself, "I can't focus on anything but getting to a level playing field. This is all I have. There is nothing else for me but Jewell Slack."

The next day Jonathan has relaxed a little. Not a tear or frown on his face. He is talking to his dad and playing cards. Breakfast and lunch were exquisite. He also cooked a huge meal that night. Jerica has a big smile on her face to see how her husband to be interacts with his father on his last day of life. "It makes me happy to see you enjoying this day Robert." Robert is puzzled but quickly straightens his face and provides a soft smile.

Someone knocks on the door and Jerica runs quickly to answer it. "No, you sit, Jonathan, I will get it. You enjoy this much needed time with your beloved father and the kids. Let me answer the door."

Jerica is back before either one of them misses a beat. "Who was at the door Jerica?" Jonathan questions her with an authoritative tone. "Jehovah Witnesses." Jerica shrugs her shoulders as the punctuation to her answer.

Later that night Jerica kisses Robert sweetly on the cheek and whispers good night in his ear. "When I was having a hard time, you were right there, you helped me, and I will forever be grateful for your compassion. I don't know why your son chose me, but I will not forget you, no matter where I go. Goodnight Robert." Staring her straight in the eyes he shakes his head no to her, almost like he knows. Puckering her lips, she answers back with a head nod yes, slow and steady. Michael looks on at the pair very confused.

Jerica lays awake in her bed as she hears silence throughout the house. No TVs playing no faint noises coming from outside and no laughter from the children as they play in the living area. Jerica's mind is going a mile a minute. "I should just let this all go. Who am I kidding, I am not this monster? Mom. Jameria. I failed. You may never see me again. God why, your message was clear. Lay and wait and I will see my out. Where is it God, I am all out of choices here. I'm broke and I need you to help me."

Jerica hears something outside her door. Slowly getting from her bed she takes a couple steps towards the door and it burst open. Jerica hearts stops beating and she is frozen for a quick moment. Jonathan and Robert both stands in the doorway one with a rope in hand and the other with a knife and a syringe.

Robert speaks first. "You can come quietly or quietly." He paused before he said that last part. "Be a good girl now." He tries to sound sweet, but his voice is as smug as his face is. Fear strikes through Jerica.

Jerica quickly turn and from her bed she pulls a gun from her pillowcase. She fires one single shot. The light from the fire is bright, the kick back from the pull of the trigger nearly makes Jerica drops the gun. She screams "did you really think I was playing and helpless? Were you coming to tie me up and keep me away? Hell, you may even want to kill me." She turns the gun on Robert who has literally peed himself.

Jonathan is hit in the shoulder. He is looking into Jerica's eyes. "Your choice, life or death Jonathan. This decision is just as easy as the one you made to kidnap me and the kids." Jerica demands he make a decision. "Because of your stunt, times up. Choose now, or I will kill him and me right now."

Jonathan pleads with Jerica to put down the gun. "I'm sorry Jerica; I didn't know what else to do. Please my life doesn't work without you and my life doesn't work without my father, please Jerica. I've worked within the limits of the roadmap of F.E.A.R. my whole life; if you trust me to create a world where your dreams are reality our life will be full."

"Jonathan I will not warn you. On two I shoot him. On three I shoot me because you do not get to make decisions for me anymore. I gave you the chance to live free with me. No answer, you make the choice for all of us. 1."

Jerica takes her aim and puts her finger on the trigger. Jonathan rises quickly from leaned on the wall and takes the gun from Jerica's hands.

At this point he is violently sobbing. Loud screams from his mountain man voice, he takes aim. The gun is small in his large hand but he pointing finger finds the trigger. Pulling the trigger and one single shot to the heart he kills his father.

The blood-stained wall and the door bearing the blood that should have satisfied Jerica. Actually, she is horrified at the hollowing coming from Jonathan on the floor next to his father's dead body. The children have not made a sound which is odd, but Jerica doesn't say a word. Her thoughts are running wild and heart rate is too elevated. This happened, now what?

"What now." Jonathan yells as Jerica, ripping the words from her subconscious. The sound of his anger makes her jump. "You do what you do with dead bodies and then clean yourself up, you may need a doctor. Me, I now can breathe and check on my children."

Jerica squares her shoulders and walks out of the room. She stops walking as she approaches the first door down the hall. There she sees Jonathan half in the room and half out as he lays down beside his father. Her voice barely a whisper, she says, "sorry for your loss". She knows he doesn't hear her because he hasn't stopped howling yet, but she says it anyway.

The next morning, Jerica looks at the calendar as she walks through the living area to the kitchen. It's February 1, 2017 and 7:45am. She starts breakfast and gathers her family. Jonathan doesn't look like he slept a wink and the kids look like they slept too well. Breakfast is being eaten surprisingly by everyone. In the dead of the meal comes a knock on the door. The voices on the other side sings out, "it's the Crittenden County Police Department accompanied by the Brussel Lands Police Department, wanting to speak to Jerica Stevenson about her mother and sister, a JoAnn and a Jameria Stevenson. Is there a Jerica Stevenson here?" Everyone starts looking back and forth at each other, but no one makes an attempt to move or speak.

EPILOGUE

There are women among us with faces with an ability to leave a lasting impression in your mind. Every woman is unique in her own way. The type of uniqueness that will have a man vowing to love and protect her with every fiber of his being. For a man to vow the rest of his life and mean every word, with solidifying actions to support is rare but obtainable.

Women are not the only ones who can fulfill a fantasy relationship. Men look and long for the type of woman that stops his heart. Someone to show off to friends and family. Someone he can be proud of and not have to worry about morally. With the right woman, a man's action, approach and total outlook on life can change. Willingly, not forced, he will take shape to her expectations.

Sometimes this can happen instantaneously and sometimes over time. Men don't know what they desire until they've seen it. Even then, some men need that one drastic thing to happen before they fully believe deep attraction and a perfect fit can be obtain in the same woman.

For a woman she has to feel it, seeing it is a first step and not even one of the important ones.

To obtain the type of the attention-grabbing love connection, a man often stumbles up on it. A woman takes time to prey on it. The problem comes in when he has to choose between his morals and his weaknesses. Women capable of providing safe territory to keep a man once he's ready are often taken by that time or so beaten down by life that all she can offer anyone are pieces that are left after someone that wasn't ready was done with her. Thick walls. This makes men have to think and actually want to get in a position to be ready to address those walls which only comes with maturity.

By the time a man is mature enough to have relationships he's destroyed many hearts. With the lessons learned he knows how to control situations that was once his demise. He's developed a sense of "know it all" because he's been there, done that. Questions that arise which are unspoken and furthermore unanswered; What boundaries are worth breaking? What consequences are acceptable? How do I choose?

Society caters to an explanation for two types of men; the perceived players that taste test women until the right opportunities comes along no matter the baggage he creates along the way and the men that put women back together as if its their duty to do so which are referred to as the mama's boys. The truth as I see it is, men don't have a reaction or direction. Mature or not. Men are impulsive opportunist. They cannot be predicted or explained.

Women are slightly sharper and grossly underestimated. For some reason men classify women as too weak or too strong and very unforgiving in all areas of life. Some men are fascinated by a woman's look of confidence while other men are intrigued by the weak parts of her that can be explored and conquered. A woman's true nature has to be tested to be discovered. Men don't see or understand the need to be challenged as a means to survival. The outcome even sometimes surprises even her. How a man reacts to situations can help a woman determine what kind of man he is and furthermore give her insight on how to deal with him.

Jonathan had a taste of both sides of the pot which brings him to a place he didn't think possible. He has a true look into what strength looks like. With his first relationship, he was

218

privy to tolerance not acceptance. That was realized when Jerica fell into his lap. In the next book in the Untraceable Identity series you will see that Jonathan has some things to change in his approach with introducing Jerica into all of his baggage.

ABOUT THE AUTHOR

My Name is Author J. LaStar. I'm a self-published author with a serious passion for growing imaginations by planting seeds of inspiration through writing. The bigger your imagination the more diverse your perspective will be in everyday situations and decisions. Creative reading and writing help dismantle the barriers we put up to define and separate reality from fantasy. An "Author J. LaStar joint" will inspire readers to challenge their reality with their fantasies by dreaming big and creating goals.

As a n author you can expect the dramatics to be entertaining and intense, but the message embedded to be relatable to our everyday lives which will encourage you to always fight for your happiness and strive for peace of mind.

Untraceable Identity deals with 2 very different views about fate. One view is that you can work hard and achieve anything, but the other view tells you if you want it you need to take it.

Visit my website for all updates concerning

Author J. L aStar

jstarpublishing.net

BEFORE I WAS AN AUTHOR

I was born Carlotta Earis Reed of Los Angeles, CA.

Since then, that premature baby girl has grown up to find a relationship with her savior Jesus Christ and her own voice through creative writing. Thankful for her son Malachi, husband Romero, sisters Carlishiea, Tranita, and Carleena, Carlotta has reached a time in her life where she is finally ready for the world to witness her talents. As this is the very first attempt to publish as a self-published author and there is still a lot to learn.

Thank you for taking this journey with me there is so much more to come.

Made in the USA
Monee, IL
09 October 2021